Table of Contents

Table of Contents (cont.)

Reading
BOROUGH COUNCIL

Reading Borough Libraries

Email: info@readinglibraries.org.uk
Website: www.readinglibraries.org.uk

Reading 0118 9015950
Battle   0118 9015100
Caversham 0118 9015103
Palmer Park 0118 9015106
Southcote 0118 9015109
Tilehurst 0118 9015112
Whitley 0118 9015115

Rea 7/09   10. JAN 11   26 M' 12.   08. JUL 14,

28. AUG 09   2 4 MAR 2011   14. JUN 12.   22. APR 15.

13 OT 19   1 6 AUG 2012

10. DEC 09   29 JU 11   12. NOV 12.   03. NOV 15.

06 APR 10.   21. SEP 11.   01. MAR 16   27. MA 16

26. MAY 10.   24 MAR 12.

18. AUG 2.   08. 2 9 JAN 2018

02. DEC 10   05. W 12.

WITHDRAWN

Author:
Title:

Class no.

To avoid overdue charges please return this book to a
Reading library on or before the last date stamped above.
If not required by another reader, it may be renewed by
personal visit, telephone, post, email, or via our website.

Library of Congress Control Number: 2009921275

ISBN 10: 0-9820562-8-1
ISBN 13: 978-0-9820562-8-8

Author's Message

In recent years, hypnosis has gained more and more acceptance as a strong supporter and part of our health system. The techniques of hypnosis are neither mysterious nor difficult. This book will give you the basics on the background and history of hypnosis. It will touch base on the techniques most commonly used for the primary concerns. Once these basic concepts are understood, you will be ready to assist yourself, or others, as you move further with your studies and your own understanding of the human mind and body.

You can receive amazing results with hypnosis. It is often directly responsible for major changes in an individual's life pattern. Even so, it is not realistic to think that every person's problem can be easily resolved with a simple approach and induction. This book will help you to pinpoint the core of the issue which will help to assist with a permanent change. The ultimate result will be in the hands of yourself or the person who is receiving the induction.

This is why proper preparation on the part of the hypnotist is so important. This book will provide you with step by step instructions for achieving optimum results from each and every hypnosis session you perform. I did my best to compile easy to comprehend information in a format that promotes understanding and skill.

History of Hypnosis

Hypnosis has a wide and varied background and few people are aware or its ancient origins. Some of man's earliest history is filled with allusions to the existence of the hypnoidal state. It's been pointed out that Cave Paintings depict humans dabbling in trances over five thousand years ago. A Grecian cult, the cult of Aesculapius, cured insomnia through apparently hypnotic trances.

In preparation for healing, a shaman adhered to certain practices that allowed his powers of concentration to be heightened. Because the shaman needed to feel focused, he would place himself in an environment that was not distracting in any way. It was not uncommon to find him in a dark, quiet room or an isolated place in the forest or in a cave. There, the shaman made himself as comfortable as possible and began his descent into what he called the lower world. This often meant visualizing an opening in the earth and journeying downward into that opening. More often than not, the journey was accompanied by the rhythmic and monotonous beating of drums, singing or chanting.

It is thought that the Egyptian priests used the sleep temples and ritualistic ceremonies to cure illness. In a British Museum, there is a base-relief from a tomb in the Thebes showing the Egyptian Hypnotist practicing his art. It's been pointed out that in the ancient Greece temple of comedy and tragedy were used for the healing of various maladies. The comedians were highly respected by the community because of their ability to use positive suggestions for promotion of cures.

The Celtic Druids used the magical sleep for various purposes. Even Hippocrates stated that cures could be effected in the ill by passes. Of course this trance state lost a lot of its popularity during the Salem Witch Trials. I'd like to note that it was recently discovered that certain "witch's salve", when applied to the skin, will cause extensive numbness and a floating sensation. This, coupled with suggestion, could easily account for the numerous reports of self-proclaimed witches that they could fly to the Sabbath on some dark foreboding night.

It was in the late 1700's that scholars, men of reason and science began to explore the unlimited possibilities of hypnosis and the practice took on credence in the scientific world. In Paris, a man from Vienna named Anton Mesmer, was producing what were to be considered impossible cures left and right through and eerie process that he labeled animal magnetism. Taking his theory and process from the core of the ancient Shamans, Mesmer, and Austrian physician, attributed his successes to an invisible force that was transmitted from the healer to the patient. He used a set of magnets to make mysterious passes over his patient's bodies. The French academy of Science admitted that his cures worked, but disputed his theories adamantly. They refused to allow him to practice in Paris. But, by the time they had managed to stop him, he had already become a big hit, popular with virtually every class of the French populous.

Mesmer would put on a dramatic show in a dark room, thick with carpets and heavy with music that would slowly crescendo into a frenzied climatic state. He would parade amongst his patients, staring into their eyes of one while touching another with an iron wand. Women were known to faint. Some would fall into a deep trance while others would cling to a huge oak tub that was filled with iron fillings and water. They would jerk and tremble as if thousands of volts of electricity were flowing through them.

But even with all the razzle-dazzle, Mesmer himself was quite sincere in his efforts. He truly believed that some unseen force was transmitting from him into his patients and that this force had curative properties.

Mesmer even felt that his powers could be transmitted into inanimate objects like the magnetic tub. He would siphon the water from the tub and provide it to his patients, professing it had curative powers. Benjamin Franklin and Dr. Joseph Guillotine (the man who created the famous beheading device) joined a few other men of science in drinking the water and declared it useless as a curative means. And, of course today, we know it was the hypnotist and not the water that was the device. Since Mesmer wasn't present at the time of consumption nor had he done an induction on any of these men prior to the consumption, it proved worthless.

But the French committee and Mesmer did discover one important fact. The healing had something to do with a person's thought process. The committee stated that the imagination played a part in the effects produced by animal magnetism.

Mesmer eventually did away with his magnets. He had discovered that he could get the same effect by staring into his subject's eyes. In a confidential report issued by the committee, there was a slight hint that in Mesmer's technique there could be suggestions or feelings of sexual attachment. Sigmond Freud also indicated that the relationship between hypnotist and subject could be likened to that of lovers. No doubt this type of thought mode led to the mounting anti-Mesmer cartoons of the day. Some of which depicted sex orgies in his animal magnetism parlors.

It was one of Mesmer's students, the Marquis de Puysegur, who discovered the role that the power of suggestion played in the healing properties of hypnosis. He was using the standard animal magnetism techniques with a twenty-three year old peasant, Victor Race. Victor was being treated for inflammation of the lungs. Instead of reaching the usual emotional and physical catharsis through the hysterical excitation and jerks so common to Mesmer's work, the young man fell into a peaceful and sleep-like state and began to talk. He spoke his troubled and even physically trembled a little as he described his impressions.

Puysegur had never seen this type of hypnotic

trance before and therefore played it by ear. He stopped Victor's tragic ramblings and began to give him positive suggestions. In this he began to inspire him with more cheerful things. This was an easy task and the peasant soon showed every sign of happiness. He began hopping in his chair and miming a song. The next day he could not even recall the visit he had with Puysegur but he did state that he felt better.

Traveling mesmerist shows toured Europe and the United States and became popular for their entertainment value as well as their sought-after healing benefits. It was in the 1820's that a Portuguese abbot, Abbe Faria, changed the way that history was to view hypnosis. He did way with the magnets, iron rods, oak tubs, and music. He discovered that hypnotism had nothing to do with the external forces acting upon the subject. The receptivity of the subject to the induction technique was the key. As a result, the Abbe Faria developed the first instant hypnotism technique. He merely clapped his hands loudly and commanded "Sleep!" The subject would immediately drop off into a deep hypnotic state!

How did it work? First, the subject had to believe in the Abbe Faria's power to hypnotize. Second, the loud clap distracted the subject's conscious mind and alerted it to the fact that something important was about to happen. And third, all senses were immediately thrown wide open and receptive so that the suggestion to sleep was strongly implanted in the subject's subconscious mind. It was only a slight variation to Abbe Faria's research that enabled stage hypnotists to cause their subjects to drink a glass of water and believe they had drunk pure vodka. Or to eat a raw onion while believing it was a juicy apple. Or even to tear off a shirt while they were frantically searching for an imaginary snake! At about the same time of Abbe Faria's research, Dr. James Braid labeled the process hypnosis, from the Greek word hypnosis, meaning sleep.

In 1860, hypnotherapy finally took root in the practice of Dr. Ambrose-Auguste Leibeault. A country doctor, he heard the presentations of Dr. Braid's works in Paris and was so impressed by them that upon returning to his own clinic in Nancy, France, he made an offer to his patients. He told them that he would treat them with drugs as he'd always done, (Chloroform had been discovered by then) or they could be treated with hypnosis. The drugs would cost them, the hypnosis was free. Needless to say, the clinic was packed with hypnosis patients!

Unlike those before him, Dr. Ambrose-Auguste Leibeault realized that hypnosis and the hypnotic induction technique was not in itself a healing device. The technique was what was needed to get in touch with the mind and body.

Dr. Hippolyte Bernheim, a physician of national repute who originally scoffed at Liebeault's research, became a student of his after Liebeault cured his patient of sciatica. Bernheim, who had been unable to cure the patient, dove into his studies.

Sigmond Freud witnessed the work of both Liebeault and Bernheim and was impressed. But in later years he rejected the use of hypnosis in his own psychoanalytic work when he found he couldn't control the fantasy aspect of the hypnotic state. When he asked his hypnotized patients to recall certain incidents in their lives, rather than tell him they couldn't remember, he made things up and recounted these fantasies as fact. Still, the neurologist Jean Martin Charcot, who gave countless hypnotic demonstrations, astounded Freud. Charcot, in fact, was less interested in the healing end of it as he was in the putting on fantastic shows for his students. Freud received a fellowship to study under him and was greatly influenced by his demonstrations.

Charcot dealt mainly with what was then called hysterical phenomena. Hysteria is a Greed word meaning "womb". It was widely believed that only women suffered from hysterical conditions. Further, it was believed that a detached uterus that had strolled over another part of the body was the cause of this condition. Removal of an ovary was the prescribed treatment for the condition until the late 1800's.

Charcot and his students believed, as did Mesmer, that hypnotic power emanated from the hypnotist in unseen rays that could influence the subject. They even went so far as to bring back the old magnetic props. Researchers like Bernheim and Liebeault were horrified at what they saw as an abuse in hypnosis. While Freud was forever influenced by Charcot's work, he ceased to use suggestions in his practice and opted for free association instead. Patients were allowed to speak about their difficulties eventually revealing the core of the problem.

In 1958, the American Medical Association (AMA) publicly accepted hypnosis as a useful medical tool. Much to the dismay of the hypnotists, they also stated that since it was being recognized as a Medical Device, they wanted only medical professionals to use hypnosis as a therapy in their practice. As a result, surgeons, dentists, psychotherapists and psychiatrists are using hypnosis in a wide variety of ways. From surgical anesthesia, to childbirth, to dentistry. It has even been reported to have been used successfully in the treatment of cancer. But what about the Hypnotherapist?

To top things off, in 1958 the AMA condemned the use of hypnosis for entertainment purposes. In 1961 the American Psychiatric Association did the same. In England and America both, it was made illegal to give a public demonstration of hypnosis on television because of the fear that people at home might become hypnotized.

Today, about 35% of the American medical colleges, 40% of the graduate schools in clinical psychology and 30% of dental colleges offer hypnosis study. And of course, there are hundreds of lectures in the field of hypnosis being held at state colleges and universities all over the US.

It is not necessary to be a physician to be a Hypnotherapist. Nor do you have to be a stage performer. A Hypnotherapist is a teacher. They teach their clients how to use a simple process that gets the body and mind communicating. They teach their clients how to better take control of themselves and their lives. That's why they're so well paid.

The unfortunate reality is that anyone can call himself or herself a Hypnotherapist. Although the AMA recognizes it as a viable medical tool, it is still not isolated as a viable business and therefore not regulated in many states. Therefore, depending upon your state, anyone who decides to hang a shingle outside their door and proclaim himself or herself a Hypnotherapist, can do so with no repercussions.

What is Hypnosis?

Hypnosis has long been associated with the strange and mysterious. Flamboyant sideshows and faith healers have succeeded in contributing to this fact. But the truth is that hypnosis isn't the least bit mysterious or supernatural. In fact, hypnotic state occurs for people thousands of times in their lifetimes. You don't notice it because it seems like such a natural state of mind. And it is! The hypnotic state is natural for all humans and many animals.

In June of 1958, the American Medical Association (AMA) defined hypnosis in its Report on Medical Use of Hypnosis as "a temporary condition of attuned attention in the subject which may be induced by another person and in which a variety of phenomena may appear spontaneously or in response to verbal or other stimuli. These phenomena include alterations in consciousness and memory, increased suggestibility to suggestions and the production in the subject of responses and ideas unfamiliar to him in his usual state of mind. Further, phenomena such paralysis, muscle rigidity and vasomotor changes can be produced and removed in the hypnotic state."

Chances are at one time or another, you have found yourself driving along a familiar freeway past your exit! Or perhaps you suddenly became aware of yourself behind the wheel and wondered where you were going. Occurrences such as these are common. This is because everything you have learned is stored in your subconscious mind. Because you have already learned to drive, your driving skill is stored in your subconscious mind. As you begin your journey, you get into your car, maneuver out onto the freeway and move into a continuous flow of traffic and reach a consistent speed. Now your conscious mind is free. That is because the knowledge required for driving exists in your subconscious, your conscious mind drifts off allowing your subconscious mind to become more active. You may become so engrossed in your thoughts that you drive in the direction of your office when your actual destination was the grocery store or the movie theater. When your attention is needed to change lanes, avoid something in the road, stop at a tollgate or slow down for an off ramp, your conscious mind comes into play again. You may have arrived at your destination and wondered how you got there so quickly!

Whenever you do anything automatic, your conscious mind is diverted from your subconscious mind and you are more likely to go into a light hypnotic state, such as the one just described. Some of your automatic activities are more apt that others to allow you to daydream. For example, your mind might drift off when you are dining alone, taking a shower, walking or jogging. These activities, like driving, are stored in your subconscious. While you are functioning in this automatic mode, it is quite easy to drift from one alert state into a different level of consciousness. Daydreaming is the first of the levels in a trance state.

Levels of Consciousness

The levels of consciousness range from a state of alertness to a sleep state. There are no rigid boundaries setting off one level from the next. Instead, the levels blend into each other and can be generally defined as followed.

Level of Consciousness	Mental & Physical Characteristics	Example Activity
Alert	1.Normal intellectual functioning 2. Normal motor response	golf
Light Trance	1. Relaxed body 2. Slowed pulse & breathing 3. Withdrawn 4. Focusing on imagined activity, or event that may or may not happen	Daydreaming about golf
Moderate Trance	1. Loss of awareness of surroundings 2. Closed eyes 3. Increased awareness	Imagining playing golf.

Level of Consciousness	Mental & Physical Characteristics	Example Activity
	of heartbeat/breathing 4. Increased senses 5. Sharper imagery	
Deep Trance	1. Greater reduction of activity/energy 2. Limpness or stiffness of limbs 3. Narrowing of attention 4. Loss of environmental awareness 5. Heightened creativity	Feel as if really playing

The middle levels are the ones in which you will find behavior modification occurring and the ones in which you will be most susceptible to posthypnotic suggestion. It is important to understand that no two individuals will have identical experiences as they progress from the state of alertness to the deep trance. One person may be far more suggestible in a moderate trance state while another in a deep trance state. It is even possible for someone in a light state of trance to accept suggestions such as numbness in a body part.

Generally speaking, when you are in a trance state in which you are receptive to hypnotic suggestions, you are apt to experience relaxation, sleepiness, rigidity or a narrowness of attention. It is also common to have a sense of strangeness or unreality. This means that you may see yourself or your surroundings in a new way, more detached or more connected than usual. As you examine the various mental and physical characteristics of the trance states shown on the chart, you will be better able to see why hypnosis has been associated in varying degrees with mystery and awe.

A Good Hypnotic Subject

Almost every living creature can be hypnotized. The process of a hypnotic technique is referred to as an induction. Two of the most important prerequisites are that the subject have a brain and a nervous system. In Mexico there is a group of Mescalero Indians who perform "gentling" on horses. A wild horse can be made gentle and tame without going through the violent bucking and kicking that you see in the western movies. This is done by approaching an animal closely and singing in low monotones gently while gently and peacefully stroking ceaselessly. It's as if a tranquilizing chemical was induced. This allows the hypnotist to ease up and lay his stomach across the horse's back with minimal, if any, reaction.

Ancient writings show that the Egyptian scholars knew the secret of paralyzing the deadly hooded cobra with the touch and making it as straight and rigid as a stick. That may well explain how the magicians of Pharaoh were able to change their sticks into snakes when Moses faced them!

In Walter Gibson's book, Secrets of Magic, he describes how lions can be hypnotized without being touched and by only the use of certain hand gestures.

Interestingly enough, a human is even easier to hypnotize. Do you recall ever driving across country late at night, tired and lulled into an unusual lethargy? Did you find yourself staring at the white lines on the road? Then suddenly having the illusion your car was standing still and the white lines were actually flashing past you? Airline pilots have reported the same illusion. When landing, they have sometimes been so fatigued that the landing strip lights appeared to be moving while their aircraft hung motionless, poised just above the runway. This is a very dangerous trance state to be in.

These are classic symptoms of hypnosis. Perhaps, in your car on a rainy day, the monotonous rhythm of the wiper blades, the tapping and swishing of the rain on the windshield and the hum of the road and engine have relaxed you into a drowsy state. Then, at a stop light, the red blinking lights of the turn signal on the car in front of you have attracted your attention and held you fixated and unmoving for several seconds. This is again a classic symptom of a dangerous hypnotic state.

Everyone has experienced this type of phenomena and it's because of that fact that it is felt that virtually everyone can be hypnotized. The only exceptions are:

1. Those whose mental capacities are diminished to the point that they are quite unable to focus their attentions.
2. Those whose are deliberately attempting to avoid the hypnotic state.
3. Those whose concepts of hypnosis are so profound that their expectations of the hypnotic state

keep them from being hypnotized unless you fulfill each and every item of their expectations.

There are four stages of hypnotic induction:
1. Fixation
2. Relaxation
3. Visualization
4. Suggestion

Although hypnosis can and is performed on those suffering senility and dementia, never try this on your own. Always refer them to a professional in the mental health field. The human mind is like a labyrinth with doors on all sides. Some doors have monsters behind them and are better left to those who have formal training and are qualified to handle the surprises that may arise.

Consider yourself a teacher and instruct your clients in the use of hypnosis as a tool to unlock the power within themselves. When it comes down to it, All Hypnosis is Self- Hypnosis. You are simply instructing and guiding them along.

There are always a few subjects who will come to you in such a confused and resistant state of mind. They will challenge you and deliberately fight the induction technique. A well-meaning but misinformed friend or relative often sends these people to you. The subjects don't really want to be there so they will respond without enthusiasm or dedication. Or the subject may have a deep-seated emotional problem that won't allow him or her to succeed with self-hypnosis. These self-destructive individuals need professional guidance that is really beyond the scope of a hypnologist or Hypnotherapist.

Instant Hypnosis

Instant hypnosis is also often referred to as Speed Hypnosis. It can be accomplished in a number of ways. In the book, Hypnotism, Dr. George Estabrooks related an experience in which he had intended to play a hypnotic record for a group of people in his home. He had told the group that he was going to play the hypnotic record and that they would fall into a deep, hypnotic sleep. Unwittingly, he put on the wrong record. It was anything but soothing! The record turned out to be a Swiss Yodeling record. As soon as he realized the mistake he had made, he quickly went to correct it but hesitated when he saw... much to his surprise... that one of his guests had already fallen into a deep hypnotic sleep.

Dr. Estabrooks discovered that a hypnotic technique is not nearly as important as the belief of a subject in the hypnotist or in the technique. Our research in the field of speed hypnosis indicates that our greatest success with instant hypnosis is in-group structure. This is because in any large gathering you will find at least a few people who are highly suggestible and they are the most quickly hypnotized.

That's the reason that most stage hypnotists call up a large group of people onto the stage. This allows them the opportunity to pick and choose the most suggestible ones from the members of the audience. A research at the University of California showed that those who are taught self-hypnosis over a period of weeks become very good subjects for speed hypnosis. Even though the initial technique takes from 30 to 35 minutes, after a few weeks of practice they could to be hypnotized or to hypnotize themselves in a matter of a few seconds.

Another way to induce instant hypnosis is to leave your subject with a post-hypnotic suggestion that in the future, whenever you say a particular work or phrase, he or she will immediately drop into a deep hypnotic sleep. It is imperative however that if you utilize this technique, especially with a highly suggestible client, that you give him or her a suggestion or a key to the suggestion that will cause him or her to go into a hypnotic sleep only when he is in a controlled environment.

The suggestion that is used more often than not is that the subjects must assume a comfortable position and deliberately count from ten down to one, going into a deeper and deeper sleep with every number that they count. That way, they must deliberately count from ten down to one and deliberately give themselves the suggestion to go into a deep, deep hypnotic sleep. Again, your client's or subject's suggestibility will have a great deal to do with how quickly they slip into a hypnotic state.

Some doctors and dentists use hypnoidal drugs. Sodium-amythol, sodium-pentathol and others can induce a state of suggestibility and a distinctly drowsy feeling. In fact some doctors and dentists use these drugs in order to induce a deep sleep before performing a physical operation or surgery. During this state, not only is the subject highly suggestible, but he or she can also be made talkative as well. Undoubtedly on some talk shows you have seen these drugs used as truth serums and they do work as such to a certain extent. Or a hypnotist will carry harmless placebos in an impressive looking container and will give a placebo to a volunteer telling him or her that it is indeed a strong hypnoidal drug; the subject will immediately fall into a deep, relaxed state. Some hypnotists have used them with great success, although the reputation of the hypnotist and the suggestibility of the subject play a great role in the effectiveness of these placebos.

Trance State

Some first time subjects will insist that "nothing happened" under an induction. This is because they didn't become unconscious or slip into a trance state. If this occurs with your subject, it's your own fault for not eliminating these attitudes with proper education. This course will provide you with a simple questionnaire that will allow you and the subject a better idea of how suggestible they are. It is also your responsibility to sit down with the subject prior to the initial induction and answer any question or calm any fears they may have.

Television, movies and fiction writers have created some very convincing myths concerning hypnosis. The average American has had little or no education in the field. Just think about how many times you have seen hypnosis on television or in the movies with the hypnotic subject depicted as a somnambulistic zombie, responding wide-eyed and puppet-like to the commands of the hypnotist?

Real hypnosis requires none of what is depicted in the theater. It's up to you as the hypnotherapist to explain in advance to your client that he or she will be quite aware of hypnotic paradigm. A good hypnotic subject will not lose consciousness. They will be aware of the surroundings and will hear sounds if they occur, but just won't be distracted by them. They should be made aware that they are able to get up and walk away if it's important for them to do so.

More often than not, the eyes of the subject are bloodshot after an induction. Some authorities suggest that this is due to the expansion of the highly relaxed capillaries (small blood vessels) during hypnosis. After a hypnotic session, point out the unusual heaviness of the limbs and give them a mirror to see their eyes if they display a need of assurance that something actually did occur.

Of course, each time the subject is hypnotized by you or by using a cassette tape or CD, he or she will find that a deeper state is induced.

Sleep vrs Hypnosis

You may find yourself using the term hypnotic sleep or your subjects will ask to be put under. This is a misstatement. The misconception that hypnosis is a sleep-like state is due to historical mistake. When Braid coined the word hypnosis from the Greek word "hypnos" (sleep), he was referring to the apparent lethargy and drowsiness induced by his fascination technique.

Not only is sleep not required for successful hypnotic induction, but it would actually be detrimental. After all, how can someone who is asleep concentrate on the suggestions you give?

Your subject's senses will become sharper and clearer in a state of hypnosis than in your normal state of awareness. It is a good idea to relax your subject's body and thoughts while you are inducing hypnosis because this relaxation quiets the conscious mind and allows the subconscious to become more active. Using visualization as part of the relaxation process has proven to be quite effective. Very few subjects remain constantly aware of their surroundings. Hypnosis is, however, an excellent sleep inducer. People who find it difficult to sleep often report that the tensions of everyday living are what keep them awake. Worry, anxiety, emotional upset all seem to conspire against sleep. The beauty of hypnosis is that it's natural with no side effects such as the ones you might experience from drugs.

With repeated use of hypnosis, one can learn to relax the body and replace negative thoughts with powerful, positive ones.   Tensions are released, breathing becomes more rhythmic and the "knots' in your subject's stomach can uncoil.

Hypnotherapists use terms like under hypnosis and deep hypnotic state Because their subjects are already conditioned by a hundred years of history and have developed a mind-set as to what they mean.

Popular Misconceptions

Some people believe that in a state of hypnosis they lose control and become putty in the Hypnotherapists hands. This misconception is perhaps the trickiest problem Hypnotherapists have to deal with.

First of all, if a subject believes that the hypnotherapist wields some occult power and that he or she must submit to it, the subject is like the owner of a shiny new car who gives the keys to someone else to drive. The hypnotherapist has only the power that is given to him or her by the subject. The notion of hypnotic power needs to be dispelled prior to working with the subject.

Another misconception is the idea that the hypnotic experience is like a drug experience, in that it leaves the client woozy, dizzy, weak or disorientated. In actuality, most feedback is that the subjects have left the sessions feeling refreshed and revitalized. It is only logical that the subject may feel so relaxed and be in such a need of that relaxation that they might need a little more prompting to become alert and aware. This is a result of their desires, not some mystical side effect of hypnosis.

The subject who is afraid that he or she may not be able to drive home or go back to work after a hypnotic induction session really has nothing to worry about because, while it's true the hypnosis is used in place of drugs during certain types of surgery, it

has not after effects other than the positive reinforcement suggestion given by the hypnotherapist.

There is an old fallacy that only weak-minded
people can be hypnotized. Actually nothing can
be further from the truth. Successful hypnosis requires the subject to be able to focus attention and
follow suggestion. A person of low intelligence or
of highly limited intellectual capacity would have
far more difficulty than a person of average intelligence would. There are some indications that writers and directors who used it for comedy effect in
their plays and movies created the myth of the easily hypnotized blithely assuring his audience that
he is above hypnosis and that nothing will work on
him, while he is slipping into a trance state. That
just doesn't happen.

One of the most respected hypnotists in our era,
Dr. Milton Erickson, reported that in over 30 experimental cases he was unable to cause his subjects to commit criminal or antisocial acts. Still, if
a person has criminal, exhibitionist or antisocial
tendencies, hypnosis may give him or her an opportunity to remove the inhibitions and play out
these tendencies.

Another unfounded tradition of concern is the
myth that if the hypnotherapist dies during the session or if he or she leaves the subject under hypnosis and simply walks away, the subject will remain
in a trance forever. Believe it or not, this all started
with a horror story written by Edgar Allen Poe, in
which the fictitious subject remained locked in his

purifying body long after the hypnotist had died! Of course it is silly, but some of your subjects will have heard weird rumors about hypnotism and the dark powers associated with it. In fact there is a high percentage of recent generation tat has decidedly mixed emotions about anyone who practices hypnosis, not to mention about hypnosis itself.

Part of your responsibilities as a hypnotherapist will be to educate the public regarding the benefits of hypnosis and the absurdities created by the entertainment media. Ignorance equals fear!

A subject will not do anything whle under hypnosis that he or she would not do while in waking state.

Dr. Charcot recorded the first proof of this fact. After hypnotizing a female subject, Charcot was called away. One of his male students approached the hypnotized woman and suggested that she lift her skirts. Instantly she "woke up" and slapped him, storming out. Although it is true that the perception and attitude of the subject can be altered. This allows the suggestions of the hypnotist to sink in and be absorbed.

Healing with Hypnosis

Let's clarify something. Doctors don't heal anything! What they do is set up the optimal conditions for a patient to get well through medication and environment. Hypnotherapists don't cure anything. They can only teach their clients to enhance the healing process. Ask you physician and he or she will tell you that no matter how hard they try, all the drugs and surgery in the world cannot effect a recovery in a patient whose mind is made up to stay sick. Conversely, miraculous healing has occurred in those whose minds insist that they WILL recover, sometimes against all medical odds.

This is where hypnosis comes in. All sorts of internal and external functions respond to hypnotic training. Blood pressure, heart rate, respiration, pain receptors, warts and other skin disorders, blood flow, the immune system and numerous other autogetic systems respond to direct thought.

In a clinic in Texas, run by Dr. Simonton, a remarkable result with cancer patients was shown when they were trained to use self-hypnosis. (Visualization and relaxation) to aid in the reduction and eradication of the cancer cells. At North Texas State University of Denton, Texas, there has been a report of increased bust size for virtually every member of an experimental group of women who used only hypnosis and suggestion over a period of weeks.

Suggestion has been used in the successful treatment of warts for centuries. Some physicians prefer to use a harmless red die and suggestions for the treatment of warts instead of caustic chemicals and surgery.

Healing & Someone Who Won't be Hypnotized

As mentioned earlier, some types of people are difficult to hypnotize. There are some Hypnotherapists who will take anyone as a client with the attitude that "a dollar is a dollar".   A true professional is more selective. This is one of the reasons you are provided with a questionnaire for the subject to fill out depicting his or her understanding about hypnosis.

If the subject is afraid of hypnosis, if the subject is skeptical of hypnosis, if the subject folds his or her arms and challenges you to hypnotize him or her, then you need to make some preliminary decisions.

Fears are usually alleviated by a little knowledge. Without going into great detail, enlighten the subject on some of the things you have learned in this course, as well as through your own reading.   It is recommended that you prepare a scrapbook with articles you have come across in newspapers and magazines on hypnosis. Explain that hypnosis is not the mysterious magic that it has been depicted as in the movies, but is more like a program of determined exercise. You are like the coach or the teacher, showing them how to do it, but the client has to do all the work. All hypnosis is self hypnosis.

The skeptic can be a very good hypnotic subject. If he or she will approach hypnosis with an open mind, you will see excellent results. It is up to you as the professional to decide whether the skeptic can be convinced enough to be a good candidate. If he or she is motivated to learn, he or she could become the best subject you've ever had.

The subject who challenges you to hypnotize him or her is rarely a good subject. Even if you succeed, he or she will only implant suggestions to neutralize your work. Remember that motivation is the key factor to successful hypnosis. There are some people whose nature is of a sort that no matter how badly they want to succeed through hypnotherapy, their own anxiety and excitement make it difficult for them to concentrate. These people can attend some small group session, allowing them the comfort of a support group and then the private sessions they may require. Another solution would be to give them a one on one counseling session on hypnosis as you totally answer their fears and develop a better rapport with them on a professional basis prior to the actual induction. Again, preparing with a questionnaire will spare you a great amount of uncomfortable and unsuccessful sessions.

In some parts of the country you will find an almost fanatical resistance to the work "hypnosis". This resistance is, of course based on ignorance. Nowhere in any sacred text will you find the word "hypnosis" and the closest thing it in religious circles is meditation (a light form of hypnosis) which is virtually embraced as a power for good.

If your subject objects to hypnosis based on religious grounds, you'll find that changing the terminology will help. Instead of hypnosis, use visualization and relaxation technique. This will allow them the benefits of hypnosis without the unfounded moral dilemma they feel they are in. Also, introduce them to the history and backgrounds of hypnosis. In short, educate them.

The Roman Catholic Church was among the first to recognize hypnosis as a legitimate physical phenomenon. They removed the occult stigma attached to it. In 1847, the Church issued a proclamation on the subject which stated in par, "Having removed all misconceptions, explicit or implicit invocation of the devil, the use of hypnosis is indeed merely an act of making use of physical media and is not morally forbidden, provided that it does not lend toward illicit ends."

In 1956, Pope Pious XII addressed a group of obstetricians and spoke of the use of hypnosis in the delivery process. (The Lamaze method is a form of self-hypnosis).

Some Catholic schools are now teaching courses in hypnosis and medicines. One example is the Marquette School of Dentistry.

The "occult" flavoring of hypnosis is undoubtedly left over from some of the flamboyance and oddities of Mesmer's day. Some charlatans still use hypnosis today as part of their repertoire of trickery. The only defense against this type of bad publicity is the education of the public to the best of your ability.

The Induction

You are now ready to proceed with the actual act of hypnosis, the Induction. There are two main techniques used in the induction process: the authoritarian technique and the permissive technique. The characteristics of each differ drastically and each one tends to be more effective in different situations and with different subjects and with different subjects.

The authoritarian technique is commanding and direct. Its purpose is to establish control over the subject and alter behavior through the use of repetitious commands. This approach was used in early experiments because the hypnotists believed that the authority they had over their subjects increased their chances for success. To some degree, this still holds true today. If the subject views the hypnotherapist as an authority figure, the subject may have a greater confidence in the induction and therefore obtain better results.

Generally speaking, the subject who are most responsive to the authoritarian technique are those who have great respect for and respond well to authoritarian figures in their daily living. People who are scientifically inclined are more likely to fit into this category than would be a highly imaginative and creative person. This technique works best in a one on one induction and is difficult to use in a group situation.

The symptoms that are best treated with this type of technique are often related to a repressed emotion. For example, obesity that started at a young age because of the birth of a brother or sister and the resulting need to gain parental attention. Since the problem originated in a childhood response to authority, the authoritarian technique is best used to take the subject back in time so that he or she can see the problem, understand it and let go of the need for the behavior that compensates for it. An authoritarian figure played a major role in the cause of the problem; therefore, another authoritarian figure can help unlock the problem and eventually eliminate it. Although again, do not try to psychoanalyze the subject unless you are a trained professional.

Any fear that began during childhood, such as fear of being alone or fear of the dark can be reduced or eliminated by regressing through the authoritarian technique. This technique works well with a subject who is responding to a mate as if he or she were a parent. As this technique is used, a suggestion is given to the subject to assume responsibility and eliminate dependent behavior. This is done during the induction by increasing the self-confidence of the subject and reprogramming independent behavior.

Here is an example of an authoritarian technique.

[Speak firmly]

You will listen to my voice and my voice will help you to relax very deeply. I want you to relax deeply. As you relax deeper and deeper you will respond to the suggestion I have given you. You will not stop smoking. You will now stop smoking. This is your wish and desire and you will act on it now!

The permissive technique employs a softer tone of voice to lull the subject into relaxation. In contrast to the authoritarian technique, the hypnotherapist and the subject are equal partners in the process. More imagery is used to enhance the suggestions and greater responsibility is given to the subject. The subjects who are the most responsive to this technique are the ones who are more imaginative and creative. Because more specific individualized imagery is incorporated into the induction, the induction becomes more real, more applicable to the subject. This technique is very successful with subjects who are striving to reach a goal, such as those people who want to become more successful in an occupation or want to improve their working conditions through their own behavior.

Here is an example of a permissive technique:

[Speak softly]

As you listen to my voice, let it help you to relax. As you relax deeper and deeper, just imagine yourself in a peaceful place. It may be by the ocean or in the mountains. Any place is fine. Imagine how great you feel in the place. Now let yourself relax deeper and as you relax deeper your desire to feel healthy and free of any habit grows strong, then stronger and soon you realize you truly are a non- smoker,

Induction Language

The language of an induction is designed to communicate opinions, thoughts and feelings. It focuses your subject's attention on themselves, their inner experiences and their body. It helps him or her to become absorbed into the realm of imagination and to communicate below the level of consciousness. The following are key components in the language of an induction:

Synonyms: Instead of using only one descriptive word exclusively, synonyms are used for reinforcement when describing the desired state. They strengthen the suggestions. For example: "You are feeling relaxed, calm, at ease, peaceful, comfortable."

Paraphrased suggestions: Suggestions are repeated and paraphrased to enhance comprehension and ensure retention. For example, "Feel the relaxation flow through your body. Feel the warmth of relaxation, relaxing every muscle in your body. Feel all the muscles in your body relax".

Connective words: connective words have two functions. 1. To maintain a steady flow so the monologue will not be interrupted. 2. To proceed in a directive, such as "and now relax, feel all the muscles relax now and breathe deeply now and just relax all the muscles in your arms and because you are relaxed, feel a warmth flow through your body..." In this context, the connective word "and" is a cue to respond.

Time designation: Words that specify time are used for stress and emphasis. They can signal the time the suggestion begins or the time it ends. For example, any of the following cues could be used to signal the beginning of a suggestion: "And now at this very moment release all tension from your body....in just a few moments you will experience total relaxation...in the morning you will awaken refreshed and relaxed. "The end of a suggestion might be signaled by "At the end of two hours you will stop studying and will end your test preparation".

The Hypnotic Voice

At one time or another you have probably had the experience of being bored or lulled by a public speaker. No matter how hard you tried, it was impossible to concentrate. You repeatedly thought yourself back to the situation and forced yourself to listen carefully to each work. Yet, quite against your will, your mind drifted. It drifted because the speaker's voice was putting you into a trance state. You were being hypnotized. There are in fact certain people whose voices have a tone, volume and lack of inflection that make them highly hypnotic.

Because the voice alone can elicit a trance state, the voice you use for your induction is extremely important to your entire hypnotic session. The voice can forceful and commanding or it can be soothing and melodic. Consider the following characteristics of the hypnotic voice.

The voice for the basic induction is usually monotone or rhythmic. The monotone voice allows your subject's attention to become inwardly focused because there is nothing distracting or diverting. The monotone is without inflection or variety in pitch or volume. It drones.

The rhythmic or singsong voice rocks you to peacefulness and lulls you into a trance. With this voice the stresses in the sentences can be anticipated. They set up a rhythmic pattern that is comforting, soothing and predictable.

There are other elements within the basic delivery that are important. Thy are used infrequently throughout the induction and can be interspersed with the basic voice, which is either monotone or rhythmic. These elements are as follows:

Use word distortion for emphasis and reinforcement: Words are sometimes distorted to achieve a special, desired effect. For example, "Feel the muscles loooooooosen and reeeeeeelllllaaaaxxxxxx. Feel the calf muscles looooosen and reeeelllaaaaxxx. They are so looooose they feel like rubber bands." This type of word distortion is particularly beneficial to use during a progressive relaxation induction if your subject has particularly hard time relaxing and getting comfortable.

Raised Pitch: The whole level of your voice changes with raised pitch. This elevated pitch, which penetrates the relaxed state of mind, has been produced by the monotone or rhythmic voice is used to give a suggestion. The pitch allows an emphasis to be placed on posthypnotic suggestions such as "and now you will stop smoking". It is also used to give a command to come up from an induction such as "seven, eight, nine, ten. And open your eyes and come back to alertness feeling great!"

Uninterrupted Rhythm: The uninterrupted rhythm is established through the use of connective words. You are pulled along the induction path by one continuous thread of speech. For example: "Feel yourself relax and continue to relax and just relax deeper and feel your entire body relaxing deeper and deeper." This continuous flow of words establishes a rhythm that pulls you into the trance and closes out any distractions. It does not allow any opportunity for your attention to be diverted.

Silent Pause: To allow time for your subject to respond to a suggestion or command, the silent pause is used. For example: "now take a deep breath...[pause]...and exhale". The pause is also used through the progressive relaxation induction. It is absolutely necessary to allow adequate time for each response. Without it your subject will feel anxious or hurried and total relaxation will not be possible.

Induction Steps

The best way to understand the art of hypnosis is to diivide an induction into steps. Analyze the wording and phrasing and identify them with the desired results.

Step one: The beginning
As you begin to focus your subject's attention on his or her breathing and inner sensations, his or her awareness of external surroundings will decrease. By breathing deeply, he or she will become aware of his or her internal sensations. You will introduce the subject's body to relaxation. The results are that the subject's pulse slows down, his or her breathing slows down and he or she will begin to withdraw and you can direct his or her attention to the suggestions you are giving.

Step two: Systematic relaxing of the body
As the subject concentrates on relaxing every muscle in his or her body, his or her mind will also become more relaxed. The subject will experience an increased awareness of internal functions and an increased receptivity of the senses.

Step three: Creating imagery for deeper relaxation
The image of drifting down deeper and deeper helps the subject to enter a deeper trance state. The tension in the shoulders is released as the "weight" is

lifted form the subject's shoulders. Any difference in his or hers bodily sensations will support the suggestion that a change is taking place. The direction [upward and downward] that is specified in the induction does not matter as long as it makes it possible for the subject to experience a change in his or her physical feelings.

Step four: Deepening the trance
In order to further deepen your trance state, a count is used that usually goes from ten to one. You count backward from ten to one as your subject goes deeper into a trance state and forward from one to ten as your subject returns to full consciousness. Although the image of a staircase is often used, you can substitute any image you like in order to enhance the feeling of going down. You may want to use the image of an elevator descending ten floors, etc.

Step five: The suggestion
Now that the subject is totally relaxed, you may begin with the suggestion for whatever therapy they are seeking. Repeating it in a manner that you have determined will be best received by him or her.

Step six: Concluding the induction
Upon completion of the induction, a feeling of well being should be suggested to avoid any abrupt return, which may cause drowsiness or a headache. Your subject should feel relaxed and refreshed. You

may want to allow some time for the subject to sit and converse or walk around a bit to make certain that he or she is fully alert before they depart.

Hypnotic Communication

Effective communication relies on the sugges-tion. Various forms of suggestion play an integral part in your daily life.

Examples:
A. You get up in the morning and stumble over your companion's shoes, which have been abandoned in the hallway. As your companion approaches, your glance slides from the shoes to his/her gaze.

The suggestion: Your shoes are not where they should be; move them.

B. You drive to work, passing a billboard showing a group of euphoric people listening to K10JOY

The suggestion: Your life will be happier, more joyful, if you listen to the same radio station these people listen to.

C. Your employer enters your office, takes a seat and says, "We're looking for someone to serve as project director and will be making a decision by the end of the month. We're extremely pleased with the way you have organized and implemented the train-ing program. You've accomplished a great deal, and have the respect of your co-workers. How do you feel about the new project?"

The suggestion is twofold: You are being consid-ered as project director and what can you say to sell yourself as a successful candidate?

D. You go out to dinner. After the entrée the waiter comes to your table and asks, "May I show the dessert menu?"

The suggestion: You are encouraged to order dessert.

E. You go home and your nine year old daughter bounds out of her bedroom greeting you with, "Wouldn't you like to hear my report on the feeding habits of the African Lion?"

The suggestion: You would like to sit right down and listen to the report.

You will notice that these suggestions vary in their degree of directness. Further, some are verbal and some are nonverbal. In hypnotic communication, you will be using both direct and indirect suggestions.

Most Common Forms of Suggestions

There are six most common types of suggestions: Relaxation, Deepening, Direct, Imagery, Indirect and Posthypnotic.

1. *Relaxation*
Relaxation suggestions put you at ease and introduce a state of receptivity why directing your focus inward. The shut out external conditions. These suggestions establish a comfortable foundation for further suggestions.

2. *Deepening Suggestions*
Deepening suggestions take you into a deeper hypnotic trance. They provide an activity that has a single focus and intensifies the subject's trance state in a number of ways. The subject can think of a deepening suggestion as a descending elevator - when a certain button is pushed, it goes down to the next floor. You can tell the subject that he or she cannot open their eyes or move their limbs.

3. *Direct Suggestions*
Direct suggestions are designed to guide you or instruct you to respond in a certain way. Direct suggestions are usually simple and to the point. They often are used in an induction that does not require the subject uses his or her imagination to any sig-

nificant degree. They are the opposite of indirect suggestions, in which imagery plays an integral part. As direct suggestions are given, the subject responds to the words rather than the images. The suggestion may be one word or several sentences that trigger an immediate response.

4. Imagery Suggestions

Imagery suggestions augment the other suggestions... They create mental pictures and set scenes that have specific purposes, such as to relax, to foster a new self-image, to serve as a "rehearsal" for new behavior or to provide an environment in which any behavior can be reprogrammed. For example, the image of a stairway augments the countdown to a deepening suggestion. Images from your past augment your recall of an important incident, which is a result of a direct suggestion. Any kind of image or metaphor may be used with an indirect suggestion, such as an image of a strong, surging river to represent a person's circulatory system or of a singing bird to represent hope. Post hypnotic suggestions are expanded through the use of images as the subject imagines himself or herself successfully carrying out a new activity.

5. Indirect Suggestions

Indirect suggestions are of two major types. In the first, a desired emotional state, such as happiness is focused on. The hypnotic subject is interviewed about his or her past and an experience is identified that once provoked the desired emotional state. Next, the subject is motivated, during the induction, to relive the experience and the positive emotions that accompanied it. A simple cue that can be used later to evoke the emotional state post hypnotically is then associated with the experience. For example, the subject may have recalled a particularly pleasant time in his or her youth when he or she was sailing with his or her father. He or she felt carefree, peaceful and joyful. The subject re -experiences that event in the hypnotic state. He or she feels carefree and at ease. A cue word is introduced that can be associated with these positive emotions. The cue word is sailing. From then on, the subject needs only to think of the word sailing in order to experience the desired emotional state.

The second type of indirect suggestion is often associated with the work of Milton Erickson. Although hew as not the first to use this technique, he certainly was the boldest and one of the most influential to give suggestions outside the conscious awareness of the subject. He sometimes used lengthy dialog to put his subject into hypnosis, told stores and presented analogies that the subject responded to and incorporated into his or her own behavior. The result was a change in the subject's experience, such as the elimination of a chronic pain or modification of a problematic behavior. For example, if Erickson were talking to a married couple who were not having successful or satisfying sexual relations, the problem would be approached

metaphorically, by talking about an elegant satisfying dinner that is not consumed all at once, but is
quietly and leisurely enjoyed. The indirect suggestion is highly in-dividualized. Each analogy, each
metaphor, must fit the problem and the subject as
closely as possible. The hypnotherapist works within the metaphor to achieve a specific goal.

6. *Post Hypnotic Suggestions*
Posthypnotic suggestions are given during the induction and carries out upon completion of the induction at a specific time during the post hypnotic
phase. This type of suggestion is used to eliminate
a habit, such as smoking or to modify behavior in
some other way such as improving personal relations at work or increasing self-confidence. The
subject hears the post hypnotic suggestion, incor-
porates it into his or her subconscious, reach full
consciousness at the conclusion of the induction
and respond to the suggestion on a subconscious
level at a later time.

Guidelines for Suggestions

There are some guidelines that should be carefully observed when you are formulating the suggestions for your subject's induction.

• *Keep direct suggestions simple and concise.*
When you are hypnotizing a subject, it is absolutely necessary for the subject to clearly and quickly understand what is being suggested .A direct suggestion should not be buried in a lengthy monologue. Many subjects respond to direct suggestions more effectively than they would to imagery. A person who cannot visualize can assimilate and act on a direct suggestion. Programming then takes place.

• *Repeat suggestions*
Repetition is important because it helps the subject strengthen and retain the suggestion. As the subject repeatedly receives the same message. The suggestion becomes instinctive. The subject acts automatically, readily and with ease, regardless of the nature of the specific suggestions.

• *Keep suggestions believable and desirable.*
Your subject needs to think he or she can accomplish the objective of the suggestions and he ore she must want to do it. If the subject doesn't believe he or she can 'do it then he or she is likely to reject the suggestion. Furthermore, if the subject thinks that

he or she can't won't really pass the bar exam, lose the weight or be an effective public speaker, then your suggestion will be only superficial.

• *Create a time frame for suggestions.*

• *Be certain that suggestions can be interpreted literally.*

• *Limit your suggestions to accomplishing one goal at a time.*

• *Break major goals down into a series of suggested incremental steps*

• *Use words that are positive, rather than negative or discordant.*

• *Avoid relaxation suggestions that are thought provoking.*

• *Use cue words or phrases to trigger and emphasize suggestions.*

• *Select appropriate images to augment direct and posthypnotic suggestions.*

• *Remove unwanted suggestions.*

Before You Begin

In order to achieve the best results from the induction, you should have a familiarity with your subject's condition, personality and habit pattern. This holds true even if the subject is you and you intend on recording the induction on a tape and playing it back to yourself.

Having them, or yourself, fill out a questionnaire with questions that will help identify patterns is advisable. When you have the completed questionnaire in your hand, spend some time in discussion about the topics with your subject to help you get an even greater understanding of their particular issue and attitude toward releasing and healing it. On each follow-up session, a follow-up questionnaire should be filled out by the subject, and again spend a little time in discussion with the subject. This will give you and idea of the areas that need to be concentrated on. Keep these files for future visits should the subject return for this issue again or for another issue. It will help you to keep a running track on their personality and pattern of response and fear factors.

The following pages contain helpful questionnaires and inductions. Follow them closely and use them for a successful hypnotic experience. Remember to take your time when working with a subject. Your speech pattern in an induction should be slow and methodical. The ... between sentences denoted the recommended places for pause and hesitation to create a stronger emphasis on what's being stated.

How Hypnotizable Are You?

While some people find being hypnotized a snap- others need a little time before it is successful. The results are up to the individual.. it is simply a matter of how well you can let yourself relax and sink into the hypnotic trance. This quiz was created by the national Guild of Hypnotists to help find out how suggestible you are.

(Circle the letter next to your answer)

1) Close your eyes and imagine yourself at a movie. How clearly can you picture your favorite actor?

  a) Extremely well
  b) Vaguely
  c) I can't do it

2) You're on a diet and bored. Ice Cream is in your freezer. You:

  a) Leave it alone
  b) Take one bite
  c) Finish it

3) How long does it take for you to fall asleep?

  a) Ten minutes
  b) Closer to half an hour

   c) At least half an hour

4) You're most comfortable traveling by:

   a) Plane
   b) Train
   c) Driving your own car

5) The boss chews you out in front of co-workers. How well can you control your emotions?

   a) I'm in control and won't lose it.
   b) I can hold it in for a while
   c) I can't control them: I lose it.

6) How often do you daydream?

   a) A lot
   b) From time to time
   c) Rarely, if ever

7) You're first off the bus and you find a wallet filled with   money. You:

   a) Take it to the driver
   b) Take it to the police
   c) Take it home and call the
      owner yourself.

8) Think about a proud moment when your friends cheered you on. Close your eyes and try to re-experience it.

a) It's easy

b) You FINALLY got it, but it took time

c) It's difficult / impossible

What's your score?

1.　10 points for each A answer

2.　5 points for each B answer

3.　0 points for each C answer

Scoring:

45-80 points: you have a good imagination and a natural for hypnosis

0-44 points: you are very analytical which can make hypnosis a challenge.

Setting up Your
Hypnosis Environment

Whether you are planning on becoming a professional Hypnotherapist, or choosing to simply apply
your knowledge to help you enhance your daily life
patterns, the environment in which you choose to
perform your hypnotic inductions should fall within
a certain criteria.

• Keep the atmosphere relaxed and soothing
    A] Colors should be calming.
    B] Furnishing should be comfortable and
        easy to relax in. A recliner or sofa work
        the best.
    C] Background music is often a nice
        relaxation aide. But not a necessity.

• Keep a recorder on hand to record your sessions.

• Keep an accurate record keeping system for your
inductions. It should be easy to pull out the files
for follow up sessions and understand the progress
that has been made.

• Make certain that whoever is answering your telephone and scheduling the appointments is fully ori-
entated on the most frequently asked questions for
hypnosis.

• Keep a scheduling book and make certain you allow time between inductions for the subject to become alert and have any questions or concerns answered before they leave.

• Have some standard post hypnotic suggestions written out on cards to give to the subject before they leave. Make certain that you instruct them on how to use these suggestions before they leave. Directions for self- hypnosis written on the back of each suggestion card is recommended.

• Although you do not want the subject to become dependent on you, it is a good idea and a comforting gesture for you to give contact information for the subject to call you in the event that they are having difficulty resisting a craving for a cigarette or alcohol. A quick booster suggestion over the phone often helps to get them through such a crisis.

Developing Clientele

Once you have your space set up and ready to go, if you have decided to become a professional, you will need to develop a following of clientele. Although word of mouth is the best type of advertising, it is often necessary to consider other forms as well.

• Local newspapers
• Magazines
• Flyers
• Mailers
• Discount coupons
• Internet web site and e-mail
• Free lectures at local clubs and organizations
• Distributing Frequently Asked Questions FAQ (see following)

Put your thinking cap on and write down whatever else you may feel is a good form of advertising.

Whether you decide to go further with your hypnosis studies and become a professional, or simply use it for bettering your own quality of living, the information you have just read forms a solid foundation.

The rest is up to you!

This collection of hypnosis inductions contains "guidelines" only and you are encouraged to shift them to fit into your or your client's comfort zone. But, in doing so, be careful not to interrupt the general flow of intent since these inductions are tried and true.

"The longer I live, the more I realize the impact of attitude on life. Attitude, to me, is more important than facts. It is more important than the past, the education, the money, than circumstances, than failure, than successes, than what other people think or say or do. It is more important than appearance, giftedness or skill. It will make or break a company... a church... a home. The remarkable thing is we have a choice everyday regarding the attitude we will embrace for that day. We cannot change our past... we cannot change the fact that people will act in a certain way. We cannot change the inevitable. The only thing we can do is play on the one string we have, and that is our attitude. I am convinced that life is 10% what happens to me and 90% of how I react to it. And so it is with you... we are in charge of our Attitudes."

Charles R. Swindoll

CLINICAL   INDUCTIONS

Stop Smoking Induction

Relax your body; relax your mind as you listen to my voice and only to my voice. All other sounds around you may be heard and acknowledged... but they do not disturb you as you listen to my voice and only to my voice...telephones ringing, people talking, cars going by, dogs barking, anything other than my voice will only serve to have a calming effect on you.... As you inhale deeply through your nose and exhale through your mouth...breathing in the clean fresh air and releasing the old stale air.... Filling your lungs completely with clean ... fresh... pure air and releasing old...stale... poisonous air. Do this breathing exercise 5 times... your heart may begin to beat strongly... and your head may begin to feel light...this is perfectly normal... perfectly alright... just continue to breathe in the clean fresh air as you fill your lungs completely...now.... Breathe at a rate that's comfortable for you.... And allow your heart rate to become compatible with your breathing...as you relax... relax... relax.... And as I count from 10 to 1...you will go into an even deeper state of relaxation... 10...9...8...7...6...5...4...3...2.. 1...

And as you are relaxing deeper and deeper, reflect for a moment on all of the success you have already had in the past...the many positive goals that you have already reached and achieved...and feel proud...proud of yourself...proud of all the positive aspects of your life... your creativity...your intelligence... Feel proud of yourself... and know without a doubt that because you have been successful in the past and because you have reached so many positive goals, you will continue to be successful in every area of your life... in every area of your life...

You are now more motivated and more determined than ever before to reject all that is unhealthy and harmful to you... bad habits... tension...stress... the habit of smoking cigarettes... you now reject this habit of smoking cigarettes... you have all the right reasons to be a nonsmoker... you do it for yourself... for you health and well-being...and that feels fine... that feels fine... and since you have been successful in the past, you will simply continue to be successful and reach every positive goal that you have and you now choose to be a nonsmoker. You begin to feel and see an image of yourself with out a cigarette or a pack near you. See yourself as a nonsmoker... you are a nonsmoker and that feels fine. You reject the habit of smoking... your mind rejects it and your body rejects it... imagine throwing a pack of cigarettes out of the window and away from you and that feels great... you have made up your mind you have mad the choice to be a nonsmoker and that feels fine...it feels fine... your body now rejects smoking cigarettes ... your lungs no longer want the poisonous fumes in them... they now want to become clean and clear and healthy once again... your sinuses want to feel clean...fresh air... The smell of cigarettes is now disgusting and the taste is unappealing and unappetizing. ... Your mouth is clear of smoke without any trace of cigarette taste and it feels fresh... your taste buds experience the appetizing fresh tastes of your food. There are no poisonous and unhealthy fumes in your system... you now choose to be healthy and strong... you choose to breathe clean air with your lungs... clean... fresh... air... you have all the right reasons to be a nonsmoker... and you have made up your mind and are now more motivated than ever to continue to create the most healthy... the most healthy and positive life for yourself... and you are now a nonsmoker... starting right now...from this moment on... you no longer smoke... you are now a nonsmoker... You feel it within. You now make a conscious choice not to smoke that cigarette and emotionally you feel just fine... you feel just fine. You are a nonsmoker... a nonsmoker... and a positive feeling will stay with you throughout the day wherever you go.... Imagine your daily routine... what you would normally be doing...see yourself..._____without a cigarette. You have new ways of dealing with old habits... See yourself in the company of others who are smoking and forgetting to smoke...because you are no longer a smoker... see yourself commanding respect and consideration for your lungs when in the presence of smokers....

Thus avoiding the perils of second hand smoke.... Your lungs wish to remain clean and fresh and new.... This is a new way to deal with an old habit and it is a successful way. It works and you feel fine...just fine... imagine your daily routine without a cigarette and there is a smile on your face and you feel just fine... whatever your destination may be...see yourself going there in your usual manner without a cigarette... breathing clean...fresh air... enjoying... enjoying being a nonsmoker. Continue to see yourself go through the routine of your day... see yourself...feeling calm... feeling as calm and relaxed as you are feeling right now... there is a smile on your face... you are a nonsmoker and it feels wonderful. You have stopped smoking cigarettes. You consciously decide not to have that cigarette... and your emotions are fine... you feel just fine... it feels fine to be a nonsmoker... imagine yourself going through a typical day without a cigarette and it feels great. The less you smoke, the better you feel... soon you will begin to notice that every aspect of your life begins to improve more and more... every day and every night... you will breathe more easily and regain a new and healthy vital energy... you are a nonsmoker and that feels fine... you are a nonsmoker and that feels fine... your yourself in situations ... see yourself in any situation...enjoying yourself...feeling great without a cigarette and that feels fine...   the suggestions that I have given you are becoming stronger and stronger... with every breath that you take and every beat of your heart the suggestions I have given you are stronger and stronger within you ... And they will remain within you and a part of you for as long as they serve you... and as I count from 10 to one... the suggestions I have just given you will become stronger and stronger within you...they will become a part of you for as long as they serve you... 10...9...8...7...6...5...4...3...2...1... The suggestions I have given you are strong within you and will remain within you for as long as they serve you... and as I count from 1 to 5... you will become alert again... you may remember to forget this session or you may forget to remember this session... it is completely up to you...as you become wide awake and alert as I count from 1 to 5... 1...2...3...4...5... Wide-awake!

Weight Loss Induction

Relax your body... take a moment and relax completely as you listen to my voice. Inhale through your nose very deeply and exhale through your mouth. Completely ... inhale... and exhale... Breathing in the clean fresh air and releasing the stale old air as you perform this breathing exercise 5 times. Your head may feel a little light and your heart may begin to beat more quickly. . This is perfectly all right... continue the breathing. Now breathe at a rate that's comfortable for you... Allow your heart rate to become compatible to the breathing ...Relax your mind ...Relax your body... relax ... relax... Now listen to my voice and only to my voice... Listen only to me and allow your thoughts to fill with what I say... All of the sounds that you may hear will have only a calming soothing effect on you ... You may hear the phone ringing or the cars passing outside or the people walking and talking. You may acknowledge that they are there... but they do not disturb you as you relax and listen to my voice.

From this time on ... Starting right now... You no longer have the urge to snack between meals... All desire to eat fattening heavy rich foods is fading away. The desire to have or eat such foods is leaving you...becoming a distant far memory. It's a past experience. It has no effect on you now. No longer do you have the desire ... no longer do you have the appetite to snack between meals. You no longer wish for late night snacks because you're already full... You're completely satisfied with the normal well-balanced meals of the day. It is not necessary to overeat at mealtimes because the well balanced meals... The moderate daily meals more than satisfy your hunger... You take pleasure in balancing, planning your moderate meals... The taste of the foods will be so sharp and clear that your appetite is satisfied like it has never been satisfied before. The tastes of your food fills you and satisfies the hunger and you find that you enjoy your food more than ever before...savor the time that you take to eat...savor the time that you take to eat. Slow down and revel in the taste and the fragrance of the foods that you eat... you enjoy the taste... you enjoy the aroma... you enjoy the food more than you ever have before... No longer are you hungry between meals, because the meals that you eat are well balanced ... and already satisfy any physical or mental appetite. Any food that you try to add to your already satisfied needs will not interest you ... and your body will not accept or allow any desire or urge to over eat... You simply will not want to stuff yourself ... because you feel much better... much healthier ... much happier... more energized ... and complete ... with a stomach that is not uncomfortably over-filled...rich heavy greasy fattening foods ... sweet foods ... sweet drinks, no longer appeal to you... They no longer matter because you only desire the clean healthy life giving foods... The foods that taste and smell better than they ever have before... Eat-ing well-balanced meals will cause your energy to be stronger... you will awaken refreshed after a good nights sleep. You will have a new and lighter figure. You will find great joy in the increased energy and you will feel stronger and healthier as you approach the final gain of the ideal weight. Marvel as your shape shifts. Look as you lose all the weight that you desire. But you lose it in a healthy gentle way. As you adjust the shape ... and the figure of your body effortlessly... without strain and discomfort... as you lose weight quickly ... without harm to your health ... and become healthier and stronger ... as you reach the ideal weight for your body ... and as you achieve the ideal weight for your body ... and have created the body you desire ... you will maintain it effortlessly ... easily ... as your mind and body are programmed for health ... only health. Never again will you eat food without thinking. Never again will you eat because you are nervous ... or bored ... or frustrated... angry ... or depressed... Never again will you eat for any reason that is incorrect for your body's maintenance... Right now ... take a deep breath...exhale...and relax... feel your body begin to adjust and transform to the perfect size and weight for you. Release the excess that you no longer need. Release...release... The suggestions that I have given you are now strongly planted...they are now part of you... they will remain with you... and remain implanted and a part of you for as long as they are useful to you...With every breath that you take and with every beat that your heart beats...The suggestions are growing stronger and stronger and your habits are transforming to new habits for perfect health and perfect weight... the suggestions are growing stronger and stronger and are becoming a part of you... you are becoming a new you... new habits... perfect health. Feel the heaviness being released from your body... Feel the peace and the happiness ... and the joy and contentment of who you are ... and who you have chosen to become...

And as I count from one to ten... with every number that I count...the suggestions tat I have given you will become firmly implanted with you and will remain with you as long as they are useful to you. As I count from one to ten you will become more and more awake...more and more alert and the suggestions that I have given you will become stronger and stronger... 1....2...3...4..5...6...7..8... 9..10 wide awake!

Induction for Depression

Relax your body, relax your mind. Inhale deeply through your nose....and exhale through your mouth. Inhale, and exhale.... Breathing in the clean clear air and releasing the stale old air... in... and out.... Inhale to the count of 8... and exhale to the count of ten, as you breathe in the clean air and let out the old.... Stale.... Air. Do this exercise 5 more times... Your heart may begin to beat stronger....this is perfectly normal... as you inhale...and exhale...and relax...relax...relax... and listen to my voice. Listen only to my voice. Now breathe at a rate that's comfortable for you... allow your heart beat to become compatible with your breathing. And listen to my voice.... Only to my voice... all other sounds around you can be heard and acknowledged as they exist while you exist, but they do not disturb you as you focus on my voice....listen to my voice. People talking, telephones ringing, doors opening and closing, any other sound but my voice only serves to have a calming effect on you. As you relax your body and you relax your mind. Now...I will count from ten to one and with every number that I count, you will become more and more relaxed...more and more at peace... more and more receptive to my words....as you relax ... relax....relax.... 10... 9.... 8...more and more relaxed...7.... 6.... Relax.... 5....4.... 3...2...1...you are now relaxed...completely relaxed... and as you drift deeper into relaxation let your thoughts relax. Relax your thought process, nothing to think about right now...just imagine yourself in a peaceful, special place ... and because your mind and thoughts are in a resting place, your subconscious mind becomes open to positive post-hypnotic suggestions... your subconscious mind is your protector, and as your protector, it will alert you to any negative thinking.

It will alert you when you are on the pat to think-ing about *insert your topic* . The moment you recognize your negative through process in prog-ress, you will immediately stop, take a deep breath and realize your negative thoughts have no value. Thoughts about _____ *insert your topic* _____

___ no longer serve you. They have no value. They cannot solve a problem, nor make you feel better. They have no value, they have no value, they have no value, these thoughts only give you negative messages about yourself...let them go. Remember you are a valuable person, you are loved and cared for, and you are smart and creative.

Now...just relax more and more and notice your breath. Just notice your breathing and refocus your awareness on your breathing and relax deeper, now refocus your thoughts and imagine positive goals, achieving positive and healthy goals... imagine a checklist of positive goals. The list may include enjoying a good night's sleep, awakening refreshed in the morning, feeling hopeful and positive about the future, feeling relaxed and calm, feeling healthy and strong, feeling productive and taking pleasure in leisure activities, like seeing friends...taking a walk, going to the movies... *insert your topic*   .

Each new day you feel more confident, you have positive goals for the future and you make good decisions daily, you take care of your health and well-being, you experience joy, happiness and laughter, you embrace the good times as well as the bad times and treat yourself with compassion and understanding. You allow your family and your friends to support you and you feel better and better every day, better and better every day. With every beat of your heart and every breath that you take you feel better and better. Feelings of negativity, thoughts of negativity are fading away...becoming a distant memory...as you feel better and better.... better and better.... Negative thoughts no longer serve you... they have no value...positive progressive thoughts are all you allow as you feel better and better every day...

And now.... as I count from 1 to 10... the suggestions that I have given you will become stronger and stronger...with every number that I count, and every breath that you take, the suggestions that I have given you will become stronger and stronger... 1...2...3...the suggestions that I have given you are getting stronger and stronger.... 4...5...6...stronger and stronger with every beat of your heart and every breath that you take....7...8..9...10...the suggestions that I have given you are now deeply a part of you... and they will remain a part of you for as long as they serve you.... And when I count from 1 to 5 you will become wide awake and alert... and you may remember to forget this session or you may forget to remember.... It is completely up to you...as the suggestions will remain with you for as long as they serve you. 1...2.... 3...4...5... Wide-awake!

Induction for Surgery

Relax your body, relax your mind. Inhale deeply through your nose....and exhale through your mouth. Inhale, and exhale.... Breathing in the clean clear air and releasing the stale old air... in... and out.... Inhale to the count of 8... and exhale to the count of ten, as you breathe in the clean air and let out the old.... Stale.... Air. Do this exercise 5 more times... Your heart may begin to beat stronger....this is perfectly normal... as you inhale...and exhale...and relax...relax.....relax... and listen to my voice. Listen only to my voice. Now breathe at a rate that's comfortable for you... allow your heart beat to become compatible with your breathing.

And listen to my voice.... Only to my voice... all other sounds around you can be heard and acknowledged as they exist while you exist, but they do not disturb you as you focus on my voice....listen to my voice. People talking, telephones ringing, doors opening and closing, any other sound but my voice only serves to have a calming effect on you. As you relax your body and you relax your mind. Now...I will count from ten to one and with every number that I count, you will become more and more relaxed... more and more at peace... more and more receptive to my words....as you relax ... relax....relax.... 10... 9.... 8...more and more relaxed...7.... 6.... Relax.... 5....4.... 3...2...1...you are now relaxed...completely relaxed... and as you drift deeper into relaxation let your thoughts relax. Relax your thought process, nothing to think about right now...just imagine yourself in a peaceful, special place ...as you relax deeper and deeper, just imagine yourself going into a deep healing sleep. A deep healing sleep.... Imagine a special healing place, it could be by the ocean, in a temple, or any place that you want. As you drift into a soothing, healing sleep, you give in to the most restful sleep you have ever experienced, and as you drift into healing sleep, you sleep sound, deep and restful and as you sleep all is in proper order...all is as it should be.

Your surgeon, nurse anesthesiologist and other medical professionals are highly competent, they are in charge and take great care of you...they watch you, protect you, there is nothing for you to do but simply relax, you are being cared for...all is as it should be...all is as it should be.

During your procedure, your Inner Observer, Guide or God is watching and protecting you. Your power for healing is activated and regulates your body every step of the way, every moment that passers your subconscious is activated for instantaneous healing. Every procedure moves along easily and effortlessly. Upon successfully completing your procedure, you continue to heal...you heal very quickly now and when you awaken from your healing sleep you will feel comfortable. You feel good and you feel as if only a few moments have passed. As you awaken and regain total consciousness you feel comfortable, relaxed and you feel as if only a few moments have passed. As I count from 1 to ten, the suggestions I have given you will become stronger and stronger...with every beat of your heart and every breadth that you take, the suggestions that I have given you will become stronger and stronger...1...2...3...the suggestions are getting stronger and stronger...4...5...6...stronger... 7... 8... 9... 10 the suggestions I have given you are now a part of you and they will remain a part of you for as long as they serve you. And now, when I count to 5, you will become alert...you may forget to remember this session or you may remember to forget this session... that is completely up to you...1..2..3..4..5 wide awake!

"The truth is that we can learn to condition our minds, bodies, and emotions to link pain or pleasure to whatever we choose. By changing what we link pain and pleasure to, we will instantly change our behaviors."

Anthony Robbins

Emotional

Emotional Release

Relax your body, relax your mind. Breathe deeply. Filling your lungs with clean, pure air and releasing the old stale air. As you breathe in and out, deeply, slowly, you begin to feel very very comfortable. And in doing so, you release all anxiety, fear and worries for your safety. You are completely and totally safe. Right now, at this very moment, you are protected and safe. No one will harm you. Nothing will bother you. You are cocooned in a web of safety that only you can remove. You are in charge completely. You are in control. You and only you take charge as you remained cocooned in your web of safety. Feel the peace and security as you relax your body and relax your mind.

You have experienced memories that have caused you discomfort, anxiety and fear. These memories seemed very real to you as you re-experienced them. But these are memories only. They are not real. They are simply thoughts of times gone by. Difficult times that are no more. Now you are safe. Now you are free. Now you are in charge.

Because you are in charge, you can choose to release these memories and free yourself from their reoccurrence. You and you alone have the power to free yourself. You and you alone have the power to keep yourself safe. You and you alone have the power to let yourself be happy, whole and free. You are in charge.

You reflect back on those memories and say to yourself... "I am in charge of my life. .. I hold complete and total control of my thoughts and actions... I choose to no longer be fearful... I choose to be safe and comfortable... I choose to release and erase these memories.... I choose to allow my body to release and erase these memories.... No part of my being will again be effected by these memories... they are set free from every fiber of my wholeness.... I am free... I am guiltless... I am painless... I am happy... I am whole.... I am ME!

You recognize as you go deeper and deeper into this experience, as you go deeper and deeper into a state of relaxation... that the memories you hold of experiences are memories that happened to a person that is not the person you are right now. They are memories that happened to a person of the past, not the present. You are a new you. You are a whole and balanced you. You are a you that is in control. These memories are in the past... they are in the distance. You fell safe and in control. You can investigate these memories in your comfort and leisure or you can release them and think of them no more. The choice is yours and you are in control.

In your waking hours or in your sleeping dreams, you feel relaxed, confident and safe, knowing that you are free and in control. You are whole and pure and safe.

You notice a quiet calm coming over you and even though you may have to see or look or investigate things that have a memory or an energy connected to them that is unpleasant or negative, you are absolutely comfortable and peaceful because you know that you are in control. You can comfortably recognize that you are whole. You smile as you recognize your skills and maturity and freedom.

You are relaxed and feeling good, and although we will end this session for today, you will take with you that sense of safety and control. As you notice your day unfolding and the next and then next, you become clearer and clearer with the realization that you and you alone are in control of your thoughts, memories and actions. You will become more and more aware of the power you have over your own happiness. You will notice more and more how safe and secure you are. You are a whole and happy being.

I'm going to awaken you slowly and easily by counting from 10 to one. When I reach one, you will awaken refreshed and invigorated and ready to continue the day.

Agoraphobia

Relax your body, relax your mind as you breathe deeply. Breathing in relaxation and releasing all tension from your body. You are sinking deeper and deeper into your inner being. A place of peace and tranquility. Relax, breathe, relax, breathe. Now, imagine a group of your favorite people surrounding you. They are warm, kind, friendly and truly giving. These are your friends and they love you. Now allow more people to join them. You don't know these people, but you know that they are just as friendly and loving and truly giving as your original group of friends. ...

You feel relaxed and comfortable in their presence. You feel protected. You could leave if you wanted to, but you really like being part of this gentle, friendly and giving crowd. They are good and decent people... You feel wonderful in their presence and you have no desire to leave.

Now see yourself moving through this crowd. As you do, your friends begin to leave, one by one. Soon, only the strangers are remaining. Notice that you still feel warm, comfortable and safe. As you remain in this crowd of loving, trusting and giving strangers and all of your familiar friends have gone.... Notice how relaxed and peaceful you still feel. Nothing has changed... you still have no desire to leave their company.

Now see more strangers join these strangers as

the room begins to fill again. Notice how safe and comfortable you feel as the sensation of relaxation and comfort remains. You smile as you realize that you are in the midst of strangers and enjoying every moment because you feel safe, comfortable and relaxed. You know you could leave if you wanted. But you choose to remain with them and enjoy their company.

From this moment on, starting right now, you will be able to pull upon this feeling of comfortable relaxation whenever you feel the need. Whenever you find yourself in a large crowd, you will be able to pull upon these sensations and feel good about being there. Starting right now, from this moment on, you enjoy being in crowds. You feel safe, comfortable, relaxed and secure no matter where you are. When you find yourself in a situation where you are beginning to feel uncomfortable or unsafe you can pull upon these memories simply by saying "I am safe, comfortable and whole:.

I am going to conclude this session by counting from ten to one. When I say the number one, you will feel refreshed and alert and ready to continue with your day.

Ambivalence

Relax your body. Relax your mind. Breathe deeply and slowly. In and out...in and out...relaxing... breathing...relaxing...breathing...relaxing...breathing (let your voice trail off and pause)

Visualize yourself at a lake. A beautiful clear blue lake. You marvel at the reflections in the water made from the lush trees that surround the lake. The beauty is breath taking and you find yourself relaxing even more. From a distance you can hear the sounds of people laughing and splashing. You'd like to investigate but you don't want to alter this comfort zone that you're in. Slowly, irritation about the conflict of wanting to investigate and not wanting to shift your comfort builds up in you. You are divided. The movement from the swimmers in the water causes it to ripple and you lean forward to see your reflection wavering to and fro.

Seeing your reflection makes you smile and forget about your ambivalence toward the swimming people and your comfort zone. You notice that the lake invited your full attention with it's rippling. The lake reflected back to you... you... the real you... and you embrace you for being there. You make up your mind that it's okay to choose, even when you choose between things of equal value. You find it's more important the you experience your decision and its results rather than standing back with ambivalence.

In your decision to act and face life with choices and decisions, you find yourself rejoicing in the pleasure of being in life and not in a state of ambivalence. There is a special pleasure you find in going ahead in life knowing that any decision you make will lead you to the next life circumstance. You notice there is no wrong decision. For every decision you make is right for you in order for you to experience that moment and the moments to follow. It's just the decision that you make to move forward.

The ripples in the lake continue and you pay no attention to anything else. Slowly the noise from the swimmers subsides and the ripples cease. You become still and smile with the knowledge that you can, do and will make all the right choices and actions with the right and perfect timing. Ambivalence is no longer a part of your reality.

I am going to end this session by counting from ten to one. When I reach the number one, you will awaken feeling refreshed, positive and ready to continue with your day.

Anger

Relax your body, relax your mind. Relax, relax... relax. Breath in clean air and breath out stale old air as you relax your body and you relax your mind. As you allow yourself to relax more than you ever have before, you find yourself in what seems to be a dressing room. As you look around, you notice that there are many mirrors.

You notice yourself in one of the mirrors and you see something you didn't know before this moment. You see that who you truly are does not reflect in the mirror. That who it is... you truly are...is only known by you. And that this knowing of yourself is still in its beginning process of exploration. You notice that others can imagine who you are and may react to the look of you, or to your behavior, or your words...but they are not reacting to who you truly are. For they can't see the real you. You fidn yourself seeing perhaps for the first time that much of your anger has been a response to the idea that people are directing their actions, words or deeds toward the "inner you." Where in fact you see now that the inner you is safe and is truly not seen.

As you take comfort seeing that much of your anger is based in a fear of being vulnerable, you now see that the outer you can easily handle upsets and that the inner you is very safe. I want you to look deeper and deeper. Look deep into that which you call "self".

Notice that what you are doing is different from who you are. You are a human being, not a human doing. The being that you are can change the doings that you do. Now, when someone says you are worthless, miserable, slow or something else... You know that if there was any truth to what they are saying it was in their interpretation of your human doing and not of your human being. You choose now to become rat more able to manage your expression of anger because you recognize that your power and strength lie in an invisible being-ness that needs to prove nothing.

You realize your strength of mind and spirit is great enough to allow you to easily regulate all negative expressions. Because you are not your feelings but *have* feelings, you can now choose who you will share them with and how you will share them. As of this minute you understand your strength is not increased with anger. Anger does not make you safe, nor is it the way for you to create distance from another. You now decide and enjoy having made the decision to see your anger, like all of your feelings, belonging to you but not being you. The next time a situation occurs that in the past reminded you of your anger or would make you angry you will say "I am not my anger, I am the manager of it. No matter what others direct toward me, it can't reach the inner me and I need not defend with anger."

Taking a deep breath, you will easily be able to decide how you want to express your feelings of anger in a non-aggressive way This feels very positive to you and leads you to wanting to awaken and enjoy your new found knowledge and skills. We're going to begin awakening now. The process continues as I count from ten to one. When I say the number one, you will awaken, ready and eager to continue your day.

Anxiety

Relax your body, relax your mind as you breathe in deeply. Breathe in and out... in and out... in and out as you continue to relax your body and relax your mind. Listen to the sound of my voice and only to the sound of my voice as you breathe in and out... in and out.. And relax... relax.... relax....

And when you are deeply relaxed, very very peaceful and relaxed, go back into your memory bank and pull up a memory of a time when you felt extremely tense and anxious about something. Pull it up to the surface and look at it very closely. Notice that as you look at this time of tension and anxiety you are still relaxed and calm. Peace permeates your whole being. The emotion seems abstract to you now.

You become pleased with yourself and find inner peace and confidence which you know has always been there, but only now is fully awakened, fully visible and present to you. You now see yourself for the fully capable human being that you are.

You notice that fear is a concept that you held onto as a representative of failure and you see now you are not a failure and things that don't wok out are being recognized as a prelude for success. You understand that no experience in life is wasted and can be utilized in future experiences and that failure is simply an idea that is fixed in time and space. You know that this is not the case with life...life just keeps unfolding... moving forward. You give yourself permission to continue living...to allow your life experiences to continue to unfold without the limitations of judgment or criticism. You allow yourself to flow with the directions your life takes, letting yourself be guided through it in a wonderful and clear manner. You rejoice in the concept of life with its challenges, successes, mishaps and rewards.

In a few moments you will awaken with the full knowledge and understanding of your worth and your strength. You will be at peace with yourself. I am going to count from ten to one. When I speak the number one, you will be alert, refreshed, excited about life and ready to continue your day.

Dental Anxiety

Relax your body, relax your mind. Take a deep breath and feel your entire body relax as you breathe in very deeply and out very deeply...slowly breathing in the calmness and breathing out the tension as you relax your body and you relax your mind and breathe....breathe... breathe...Starting today, beginning right now, you will transfer this feeling of deep relaxation and comfort to your experiences in a dental office. Your mind has the capacity to stimulate certain chemicals in your brain. One of those chemicals that your brain produces is endorphins. Endorphins are a group of proteins with potent analgesic properties that occur naturally in your brain. They have documented endorphins as being much more powerful than morphine and your mind has the ability to produce them. When your mind releases these proteins, you experience a calm, utopic response. That is, a response where you are in complete calm and relaxation, very positive and up-beat.

The next time you visit your dentist you will pull back this experience and notice that all the stress, anxiety or fear that you normally experienced is leaving you as your brain generously releases endorphins. Say to yourself "I release, I release, I release" Your mind will relax... your body will relax. You will be able to conduct yourself in a calm, pleasant state of mind. The dental procedures will be conducted efficiently and quickly. The time you spend in the dentist's chair will seem to go quickly because you are now engaging in the endorphin response while you relax in the dental chair.

At all times you will be able to engage in a coherent conversation, follow instructions and feel totally calm and comfortable. You are now planting the ideas firmly into your subconscious mind that you can be comfortable when you are at the dentist office. You can be relaxed during any and all dental procedures. You are in control. The past is not the future…it is gone… the future is what matters and your future is that of relaxation and pleasure during each and every visit to the dentist. Your negative experiences and fears from the past are now drifting away. They are being replaced by these positive, healthy suggestions. They are being implanted firmly into your subjective mind, melting away any fears that you had and turning them into distant memories. They have been replaced with these positive suggestions and responses and these positive suggestions and responses will surface each and every time you visit the dentist.

The suggestions I have given you are firmly implanted into your subconscious mind and can be brought forth with the word "relax". I am going to count from ten to one. With every number that I count, the suggestions that I have given you will become more and more firmly implanted in your subconscious mind. When I reach number one, the suggestions that I have given you will be deeply rooted in your subconscious mind, ready to be called upon at will. You will be confident that you are in control. You will feel refreshed and happy and ready to continue with your day, knowing that you and you alone are in control.

Fear of Animal(s)

Relax your body, relax your mind as you breathe out any tension that my be harboring itself in you. And as you continue to relax your body and your mind I want you to place yourself in midst of a beautiful zoo. See the animals both big and small within the confines of the zoo. Look into their eyes. You can see how docile they are. Now, I want you to go even deeper into the thoughts of these animals. What are they thinking? Are they feeling aggressive and wanting to hurt you? No... Quite the contrary... they are feeling that they want to just live and let live.

This is often the thought process of other creatures on this planet. They want to just live and let live. They don't think of hurting, just surviving. They don't kill for sport, as we humans do...they kill for food and survival. They hurt and kill only if they feel like you may hurt or kill them. Do you plan on hurting or killing them? Absolutely not.

You realize that since you represent no harm to the, there is no reason for you to fear them. For without the threat of harm, they pose no threat to you. You sense the love for life and freedom that they possess. A love for life and freedom that is similar to yours. You recognize the commonality between you. You recall that it is written that we humans have dominion over these creatures. As you keep this in mind and continue to tune into their feelings and thoughts the fear that you had for them is transmuted into compassion and love.

You understand that there are times when an animal is filled with its own fear and anxiety and isn't always able to see through it and my pose a threat at times. But this is rare indeed. And you trust your inner senses to notify you of a situation like this so that you can avoid it. But for the other 99% of the animals who simply want to live and let live, you feel a growing bond.

See yourself walking up to the cage doors of these animals and one by one letting them out to meander amongst each other and you. Notice how calm and peaceful you feel as you caress the head of a (animal that client is fearful of). Feel the bond and love as you make friends with all of the creatures of the zoo. Now, guide them all out of the zoo and into a great open field. There are no barrier there. Simply a great wide space for all to co-exist. You notice that you are the leader, which reminds you that you have dominion over all other creatures. You notice how peaceful and tranquil you feel inside as you lead these animals to the open field. As you approach the field, you notice that it contains domestic animals as well. You see a fearful dog snarl and you smile at it with love and affection. The natural instincts of the dog allow it to sense your friendliness and bonding and it comes to lick your hand. You smile with love and appreciation as all of the animals from the zoo mingle peacefully amongst the domestic animals and you realize that we are all children of the earth and we don't need to be afraid of each other.

This new found courage, bonding and peace will stay with you long after I have counted to ten. When I count to ten, you will become alert and refreshed, while feeling peaceful and happy and ready to continue with your day...knowing that you are in control always and that you have no need to fear animals that you have dominion over.

Fear of Flying

Relax your body, relax you mind as you breathe in and out, slowly...slowly. Breathing in the fresh and clean air and releasing the stale old air. And as you become more and more relaxed and you breathe at a rate that is comfortable for you we are going to go over your travel plans. If you should feel uncomfortable and any time during our review of your travel plans, simply raise your finger and we will shift our progression.

Now, imagine yourself at your home. You are comfortable and getting ready for your trip. See yourself going over your packing list and checking off the things that you have already taken care of. Imagine yourself completing the packing of your suitcase and locking it. See yourself making certain that all the preparations are in order. You feel confident, relaxed and ready for your travel adventure. Now, see yourself placing the luggage in a car and getting in. You have allowed a car to pick you up and take you to the airport so you sit in a very relaxed fashion as you allow the car to take you to your destination.

Traveling in a car is very familiar to you and you are at ease, feeling calm and secure. See yourself arriving at the airport and getting out amongst the other travelers. See yourself collecting your luggage from the car and the skycap helping you to check it in. As you hold the receipts the skycap has given you for your luggage, notice how calm and peaceful you still feel. You stroll in a relaxed manner into the terminal and stop at the security check. You already have your ticket so you sit calmly and await for the boarding announcement.

See yourself going into the boarding area and approaching the counter at the gate to check in and verify your seats. The attendant at the counter may stamp your ticket and take it at this point, or he may simply check their records to verify your place. If the plane is not too full, they may say you don't need to check in at all since you already have your seat assignment. You are still feeling relaxed and comfortable.

A few minutes prior to flight time, they begin to board the plane. Notice how relaxed and at ease you are as you step in line to board. You settle in and get comfortable in your seat. You may wish to have a book or magazine with you to read during this time.

The other passengers get comfortable and seated in their seats and then the attendant go over the standard safety precautions and you notice that many of the other passengers are so seasoned with traveling in this modality that they pay little, if any attention to the attendant. You relax and listen to the announcements. You take special notice of how many rows there are to the exit doors and you make certain your seat back is in an upright position for take off. You know you will be able to recline your seat later, after the plane is in the air and the pilot give the signal.

Think about how closely the plane resembles a car that took you to the airport. It has wheels, it has windows and it has a driver. The pilot is just as comfortable in flying the plane as your car driver was. As the plane taxies down the runway you are reminded of how your car taxied around other vehicles on its journey to the airport. The plane backs out of the boarding area similar to how your car backed out of your driveway. Your car pulled onto the main road and the plane pulls onto the runway... You have driven uphill many times into the mounts and the take off of the plane reminds you of those times. Again, comparing this to a ride in a car...the plane is airborne and you are now simply sitting back and relaxing just as you would in a car as you await arrival of your destination.

Soon the lights go on informing you that you not only can unbuckle your seat belt, but that you are free to move around if you desire. You smile at this and recognize that this is an advantage that you don't have when riding in a car.

When it is time to land, you will need to have your seat back upright, your tray table in the stored position and your personal belongings either in the overhead storage compartment or under the seat in front of you. The attendant will help you if you need it. Imagine yourself ... comfortable, calm and relaxed as you put your seat in an upright position and make certain your seatbelt is fastened securely. See yourself remaining calm, carefree and relaxed as you go this. Notice that you didn't even mind the announcements at the end of your flight. Note how excited and satisfied you are to have reached the end of your journey. You were in complete control of your emotions, behaviors and reactions. The attendant quickly says good-bye to you as you leave the plane. See yourself getting off the plane and retrieving your luggage from the baggage claim area and, if you intended to meet family or friends... see them waiting there eagerly for you.

The suggestions I have given you are now firmly implanted in your mind and they will remain there until they no longer serve you. As I count from ten to one, the suggestions that I have given you will become more and more firmly implanted in your subconscious. They will be available to you whenever you choose simply by you stating the word "relax". As I count from ten to one the suggestions that I have given you are strong and permanent until you no longer wish to have them there, because you are in control. When I say the number one, you will feel refreshed, relaxed, alert and happy... eager to continue your day and looking forward to any future flights you may have.

Fear of Job Performance

Relax your body, relax your mind as you breathe in to the count of eight and out to the count of ten...again.... again... again... (pause while the client breathes) as your body relaxes and you have a sense of going deeper and deeper down into your inner being.

Take a moment to remember a time when you were driving a car and navigating through traffic while engrossed in a conversation with your passenger. Or the time you talked on the phone while making dinner... and so on. Recall how well you performed both tasks. You perform many things well. Especially those activities that you have done several times before. You have the capacity to perform multiple tasks simultaneously while keeping a calm and level head.

Each time that you perform a new task, slow down and take your time. Make the effort to do each element of the task well. You will increase your speed when you have fully mastered a task. There are always levels of performance within levels. How you perform a new task now is very different from the way you perform in the months to follow... Or in the years to follow.... Allow yourself the time to grow on the job. Feedback from other workers can be of great value. Encourage and allow them to offer it whenever it is beneficial and constructive.

You may find out, by sharing your experiences, that there are many ways of completing the same job. With an awareness of more options, you have greater flexibility. This greater flexibility will help to gain more confidence and competence. Other people instructing or inspecting your work only inspire you to do your best.

Remain alert, but receptive. Do the best of which you are capable. In time, your abilities will improve and your reflexes will quicken. You will increase the quality of your work. Others know that too. They have also been through the same learning process. Just by acknowledging this fact will create a great relief and freedom from stress. You have the abilities and are capable of performing your job well. Others saw it when they placed you in that position. Others understood that there would be a learning curve with this job as there is with all jobs. You too understand this and allow yourself the freedom from stress. You allow yourself the time to move through this learning curve. You are confident that you can do this job, just as others are confident that you can do this job.

When I count from ten to one, you will awaken and feel positive and ready to go to your job and give it your all, knowing that you will progress and improve with every passing day. When I say the number one, you will awaken fresh and alert and ready to continue with your day.

Fear of Public Speaking

Relax your body, relax your mind as you listen to my voice and only to my voice. No other sounds will disturb you as you listen to my voice and you relax your body and you relax your mind. Take a deep breath and let it out completely....again.... now I would like you to think strongly the mental affirmation that you have something to say. This is something very worthy, that will enrich and enlighten others. See yourself poised, confident, calm and serene as you recognize a desire to express your ideas to others.

See the people eager to hear what you have to say. See them gather seated before you with genuine interest. Remind yourself that it's okay to feel a little nervous prior to speaking in public. Many famous speakers have reported slight "butterflies" prior to giving a speech. Breathe deeply and allow those butterflies to be released.

Just before you speak, take a moment and think of exactly what you are going to say. Then review yourself as you have practiced vocalizing your thoughts in the past. Perhaps you practiced in front of a mirror or with a tape recorder. You have prepared yourself, organized your thoughts and chosen the words that you wanted to use to express your thoughts. You are now very confident, calm and relaxed. Every day, two or three times a day, I would like for you to pause in what you are doing...relax yourself and state these mental affirmations... "I have something worth sharing with other. I can express myself clearly and precisely... I get pleasure from expressing my thoughts and concerns with others just as they get pleasure in hearing them. I can be poised and confident when I express my thoughts and concerns."

Do this exercise slowly, quietly and with feeling. Hear yourself speaking clearly and precisely. Notice how the words and sentences flow from you in audible and concise tones. Notice that your ability to "think on your feet" has improved ten fold. You find that every time you speak publicly you learn something new about you and your abilities. You learn something new about you. You learn something more about the group you are sharing your thoughts and concerns with. You are enjoying the experience of public speaking.

I am going to count from ten to one. When I reach number one, you will feel refreshed and alert and excited about the prospect of any and all public speaking opportunities you may have.

Self-Esteem

Relax your body, relax your mind as you breathe in slowly, deeply...filling your lungs with pure and clean air. Now exhale, slowly...very slowly... and as you exhale, feel all tension, anxiety, fears, worry, and dis-ease of any type leave your body. Again..... allowing yourself to go deeper and deeper down into your inner being. As you go deeper and deeper down into your inner being you become more comfortable with yourself and you begin to pay particular attention to that inner part of you. The inner part of you that at first may seem more of a concept than an experience. But... as you listen carefully to the suggestions that I am giving you, you notice that there is within you a kind of light... a kind of source of goodness, energy and light. Take your time. This may seem difficult at first, but as you breath in and out and become more and more relaxed, you will see more clearly the inner you and be more comfortable in the presence of the inner you.

It becomes clear to you as you go deeper and deeper and feel better and better, that who it is that you really are has yet to be discovered. You realize that who you are is far greater and far more spectacular than anything that life's experiences has allowed you to reveal. You begin to see now in a way you have not seen before. It becomes clear to you that all of your evaluations of yourself and your assessments of yourself have included very little real information of you. You suspect, as you go deeper, that there is so much more with you than you ever had a chance to express or share and you are excited to bring this part of you to the surface of your being. No longer will it lay in wait of discovery. The time is now to bring it forth and allow the real you to be known, not just by you, but by all. You are realizing the great value in this "more of you". It's a greater value than any accomplishment or any particular thing in life that you have done.

From this moment on, each day you will set aside time where it is okay for you to go back into this very special state, where you can recognize and focus on the person that you really are... as you do this, the person who you really are will become clearer and clearer to you.

You are a magnificent human being, alive, fully awakened inside, whose heart is great and full of love ready to share. There is no limitation within the being that you are. There may be imposed limitations as to how it is that you can express yourself according to the tools available and the experiences that you have, but those are "imposed" and don't reflect the true you. "Imposed" limitations have weakened walls and can be broken through with desire, knowledge and positive actions. You are not intimidated by them.

You are an expression of love. You are an expression of life unbounded. Each and every day you discover more fully how all of you functions and how all of you can be expressed more and more fully and beautifully. You are a being of perfection. You notice that you need less and less from others and can provide more and more from yourself, for yourself. You also notice and will notice with each passing day that because you are much more able to nourish and nurture yourself that all of your relationships go more smoothly and you are able to receive love and give love far more comfortably than you may have ever been able to do in the past.

I am going to count from ten to one. As I count from ten to one, with each number that I count, the suggestions that I have given you will become more and more a part of you. When I reach the number one, the suggestions that I have given you will be firmly implanted within your being, you will feel happy and positive, energetic and refreshed and ready to continue with your day.

Medical

AIDS

Relax your body, relax your mind as you breathe deeply... filling your lungs with air....breathe in to the count of eight and out to the count of ten. Deeply, slowly...as you relax your body and you re-lax your mind... relax...relax...relax....

Think of a place that you have been that you found to be the most beautiful place that you've ever seen. Begin mentally to stroll through this beautiful place. Mentally walk through this place. As you are walking, you notice there is an escalator hidden in the far corner. Once you have reached the escalator, get on it and allow it to begin to move slowly. As the escalator moves slowly you begin to descend down. Down.... Down... down... down... When you finally reach the destination and the es-calator comes to a stop, you will notice a doorway before you. Got to the doorway and gently push open the door. Enter through.

You now find yourself in a laboratory. It is bril-liantly lit, making visibility extremely easy. Against the far wall is a large screen, like a large movie screen in a theater. Directly in front and facing the screen are three chairs. Two of these chairs are slightly below and in front of the third one. The third chair, which is behind the other two and slightly elevated above them is larger than the others. On the arm of the larger chair is a small keyboard.

You sit in the large chair and type on the small key

boards the words "My Body". ...

Immediately, an image of your entire body will appear on the large screen. On your left arm of the chair are two dials. One of them will rotate the picture to any view you choose, simply by turning the dial. You are able to manipulate and rotate the picture to any angle, any view that you'd like to examine. Just below that dial is the second dial. This dial magnifies. By turning it you can magnify the picture large enough to show even the smallest particle and then return it to normal size. Any view of your body that you may choose to see is available to you on this screen.

If you would like a heat sensitive picture of your body, simply type in the words "heat picture" on your keyboard and the screen will produce an image that will show the points of heat and cold throughout your body. If you would like to view your energy systems, type in "energy picture" and the screen will show the energy flow and how it circulates throughout your body...and so on.

After a moment, two people enter the laboratory and approach the two chairs below the one you are seated in. When they enter, they introduce themselves to you, so you'll know who they are. They are there to advise you. You are in complete control. *you* are in complete control. You are the one who will make all of the decisions... they will simply advise you. Perhaps with information that you may not normally have access to.

In this laboratory every chemical, every tool and

every device that you could ever need or use to enhance your state of well being is available. Everything you need is here to assist you in the healing
of your body and mind. To help you achieve your
goal of total wellness.

If there's a specific part of your body that you
would like to see on the screen, simply type in the
name of that body part. Such as your left ear or
your right eye... whatever part of your body that
you feel needs attention. You can type in a single
body part or a large group of body parts, such as
"digestive system".

Then with the tools, devices and chemicals in the
laboratory and the advise of your assistants, you
can begin to remove any state of dis-ease. You may
wish to cut out or burn away or cleanse things or
parts of your body that are creating the dis-ease. If
you cut out a toxic body part, such as a lung or a
liver, the miraculous equipment in the lab will allow you to immediately replace that body part with
a fresh, new and compatible body part. You may
choose not to cut it out, but simply cleanse it with
the chemicals and equipment the laboratory pro-
vides. You are in control and the choices and options are yours to select from.

There is not pain. There is no destruction of
healthy tissue. Trust your intuition... trust your
intuition. Use images that come to you regarding
how best to assist your body in its healing process.
Trust your intuition.

As I remain silent for a few moments you can take

the time to survey your own body and perform the necessary healing on it in this laboratory. When I rejoin you, it will not startle you......

(silence for a specific period of time)

Now, I am rejoining you. As you complete your healing session on your body, you remember that each healing image, each thought of renewal and revitalization sends messages of health to those inner centers that control your state of wellness. Heal now.... Heal...now... Thank your advisors for their assistance and give thanks to your body for responding to the healing that you provided it. I will be silent for a brief moment to allow you the opportunity to do this. (slight silence)

Now, I am going to count from ten to one. When I count to one, you will feel rested, renewed and satisfied that your inner-healing process has taken place. When I count to one you will take a deep breath and awaken satisfied, healthy and refreshed.

Burns

Relax your body, relax your mind... relax...relax.. as you listen to my voice and only to my voice...relax your body and relax your mind... relax... relax... as you listen to my voice and only to my voice. Breathe in slowly... as you exhale... all pain and darkness is released with the stale old air. Breathe in to the count of eight and out to the count of ten.

As you allow yourself to become more and more relaxed and more and more comfortable, you notice that with each breath that you take your circulatory system in your body is becoming more and more efficient. Your immune system begins to function in a perfect and precise manner. Your brain sends a message to each and every part of your body, to each and every cell of your body, is that complete and total healing can and will occur. Rapidly, gently, completely healed. This message is being heard by and responded to by all parts of your body. Every system in your body that is responsible for its healing is coming to attention and responding to the command of complete and total healing.

Those areas of your body that have experienced burn are now experiencing increased circulation and a level of increased healing. There is no opportunity for infection. There is no pain. Only complete and total healing.

You understand that your mind controls your entire body. That your thoughts control your reality.

You also understand that you control your mind. You control your thoughts. You choose to heal and because you choose to heal you simply need to direct you mind on this matter and it, in turn will direct your body. It is not complicated...it is not difficult.. it is the natural order of things. You and you alone are in control of the healing process of your body and you choose to heal completely and totally right now. Right this minute.

Relax and get quiet as you feel the sensation of your body responding to these commands. Recall your body as it was prior to the burn experience. Recall how easily and comfortably you moved prior to the burn experience. Remember the wholeness of your body prior to the burn experience. Now, instruct your mind to bring back that condition. Instruct your mind to bring your body back to that state or a state better than that state. You are in control and have the power to instruct your mind in any way you choose. You choose to instruct it to heal your body totally. Completely.

Your body remembers this state well and quickly responds to the command to return to it. You are comfortable, pain free, scar free. Totally healthy and whole.

Now, I'm going to count to the count of ten. When I reach the number ten you will awaken feeling peaceful, positive, healthy and renewed. When I count to the number ten you will awaken ready to move forward in life.

Cancer

Relax your body, relax your mind... relax...
relax.. as you listen to my voice and only to my
voice...relax your body and relax your mind... relax... relax... as you listen to my voice and only to
my voice. Breathe in slowly... as you exhale... all
pain and darkness is released with the stale old
air. Breathe in to the count of eight and out to the
count of ten.

Continue to relax even deeper. As you do, I'd like
you to imagine that there are two layers of you. Your
duplicate body is projecting away from your main
body. Both bodies are you. See yourself hovering
over your body and then climbing into it...down...
down... down.. as you get smaller and smaller. You
are growing smaller and smaller as your thoughts
turn inward and you become smaller and smaller
until you are no larger than a single cell.

Now that you are the size of a tiny cell you are
able to weave your way through all the tissues of
your main body. You are now able to seek out the
weak yet destructive cancer cells that are raising
havoc within your body.

You carry with you a bag of tools, chemicals and
electrical devices. You set out to find these cancer
cells and destroy them with the tools, chemicals
and electrical devices that you have in your bag.

Look deep within your body for these cancer
cells. When you find them, investigate them close-

ly. Look for clues that will tell you what you need to use to neutralize and destroy them. I will remain silent for a short period of time to allow you to do this. When I rejoin you, it will not startle you.

(Bried Silence)

Now that you have taken time to find these cancer cells and destroy them take pride and pleasure in knowing that you are healed and whole. Understand that you are totally in control of the health of your body. You can decide to allow dis-ease to enter and remain or you can allow only ease in your existence. You are in control. Should you allow dis-ease to enter and then change your mind... you have only to make the decision and remove the dis-ease. The power is within you. The power IS with in you. The power IS within you. You have chosen to remove the destructive cancer cells from your body... therefore they absolutely can not remain. Nothing can remain in your body without your permission. You are in control... you are in control... you are in control...

Now, I'm going to count from ten to one. When I count to one, you will awaken refreshed and renewed and ready to continue through life in a healthy and whole body.

Colds or Flu

Relax your body, relax your mind... relax... relax.. as you listen to my voice and only to my voice...relax your body and relax your mind... relax... relax... as you listen to my voice and only to my voice. Breathe in slowly... as you exhale... all pain and darkness is released with the stale old air. Breathe in to the count of eight and out to the count of ten.

Your body has a wisdom that your conscious mind is not always aware. Right now, the stuffiness, the upset stomach, the headache and fluctuations of heat and cold that you are experiencing are actually your body's way fighting off a cold or flu that don't need to be experienced. There is no reason for you to be uncomfortable while your body heals itself and rids itself if any dis-ease.

Relax your thoughts, relax your mind as you allow yourself to go deeper and deeper into your body and know that you absolutely do not need to be the slightest bit uncomfortable while your body fights off a cold or other dis-ease. Allow your mind full visions of health, healing, comfort and peace. Imagine one, pure, perfect color and imagine that color mixed with a sound or vibration starting at the top of your head and slowly flowing down to your feet. Then back up to your head...then down again in a gentle, rhythmic pattern. Cleansing, healing, repairing, coating every fiber and cell of your body with just the right balance.

Feel your body get comfortable and relaxed as it sheds all dis-ease and the illness drains away and the light and sound break up any congestion, increase your circulation, decreases inflammation. You are calm, peaceful, serene and tranquil as you allow your body to shed all illness and dis-ease. You allow the healing process to take place from a point of comfort.

I am going to count from ten to one. When I count to one, you will awaken feeling the healing process in motion and renewed and ready for complete and total health and the joy of life and living.

Colitis or Intestinal Irritation

Relax your body, relax your mind... relax... relax.. as you listen to my voice and only to my voice...relax your body and relax your mind... relax... relax... as you listen to my voice and only to my voice. Breathe in slowly... as you exhale... all pain and darkness is released with the stale old air. Breathe in to the count of eight and out to the count of ten.

Now, continue to relax as you begin to erase any pain or discomfort from all parts of your body. Feel the energy flowing through your intestines in a comfortable and relaxing manner.

Now imagine your intestines in your mind. See them all knotted and knurled from the tension and the colitis. Now...see yourself smoothing out these intestines so that they rest within your abdomen in a smooth and healthy manner. See a golden fluid being pushed throughout your intestinal tract. Starting at you stomach, it flows throughout your small intestines and into your large intestines. As it flows, slowly...steadily... it repairs and relaxes the walls of your intestines. In doing so, it allows your intestines to again work in a healthy manner.

No more will you experience sporadic functioning of your intestinal tract. No longer will you experience cramping or any other sign of discomfort. Did-ease does not exist in your body. You have chosen to heal yourself and you will remain healed for as long as you choose to be healed. You have complete and total control over the health and well being you're your entire body. Every cell in your body is subservient to your command. You need only speak or think yourself to be well, with pure intent and belief and you are as you speak and think. You have chosen to release all dis-ease from you body, and it is so and will remain so for as long as you choose. You are in control. You are in control. Now, take a moment to ask yourself what it was that caused you to allow your body to accept this dis-ease in the first place. Take a moment to think long and deep into your subconscious. It may not be apparent at first. Take your time and think. I will remain silent until you raise your right index finger to indicate that you have determined the cause.

(brief silence)

Okay... now that you have determined the root of the matter...see yourself opening a door and tossing this root out. Now, close the door and turn your back, never to open that door again. You are in control. You can choose to allow this cause to return or you can choose to never allow it again. You are in control. You are in control... you are in control.

Now, I'm going to count from ten to one. As I count from ten to one, you will feel your determination and healing growing stronger and stronger. You are healthy, balanced and whole. As I count to number one you will awaken refreshed and renewed and ready to continue with your day.

PMS

Relax your body, relax your mind. Breathe deeply. As you being to breath, allow yourself to release all the negative that is holding you back from receiving your good.

As you release all the tension in your body, you also release all worry and fear. Whether you are aware of this worry or fear is not important. Release it and allow it to flow from your being.

The circulation in your body is increased and improved. As your body's circulation increases and improves it allows you to cleanse yourself. Relax as your body becomes perfectly balanced. You feel your abdomen respond to this cleansing and balancing as it relaxes more and more. And as it relaxes more and more, you release from it anything you may have been holding in that is toxic or negative. Feel health and ease flood through your abdomen as you release all dis-ease.

Anything that you have been holding that might be connected to this dis-ease is leaving you. You are left with your body feeling complete, balanced and whole.

You are comfortable and free...Able to work

perfectly in a balanced and complete manner. You are clear from all toxins and negative energies. Your body is returned to the perfect whole. You give yourself permission to have every aspect and dimension of your body free from dis-ease. You function perfectly.... Your abdomen falls into balance with the rest of your body, allowing you freedom from dis-ease and the ability to function in a perfectly balanced manner. Your body is whole, comfortable, balanced and functioning with no undue difficulty or discomfort. Feel the comfort. Feel the freedom and the balance. Feel the ease.

You will remember these words whenever disease begins to creep back into your body or your reality. You will remember these words whenever needed and when you do, you will enjoy the feelings and sensations of relaxation, peace and harmony. You will reinforce this by repeating the words "peace, harmony, balance, relaxation"... "peace, harmony, balance, relaxation"... "peace, harmony, balance, relaxation". And as you repeat these words you will become more and more at ease. Your whole mind/body system will function with ease and balance. Smoothly. Perfectly.

I am going to awaken you by counting very slowly from ten to one. When I reach the number one you will feel refreshed, alert and free from dis-ease.

Spiritual

Fear of Ghosts

Relax your body, relax your mind... relax... relax.. as you listen to my voice and only to my voice...relax your body and relax your mind... relax... relax... as you listen to my voice and only to my voice. Breathe in slowly... as you exhale... all pain and darkness is released with the stale old air. Breathe in to the count of eight and out to the count of ten.

Now that you are feeling relaxed and calm, visualize a stairwell ... a very well lit stairwell. Now, see yourself walking down the stairwell. You may not see me near you, but know that I am with you while you walk down the stair well. Watch your feet as you walk down the stairwell. There is a railing that you can hang onto if you choose to do so. And as you walk down the stairwell I am going to count from twenty to one. With every number that I count, you will walk now one more tread. When I reach number one, you will be at the bottom of the stairwell. Let's begin... 20...19..18.. (etc.)

Now that you are at the bottom of the stairwell, you see before you a long corridor. Walk to the end of the corridor. When you reach the end of the corridor, you will see a beautiful gilded doorway with a beautiful golden door knob. Place your hand on the golden door knob and turn it slowly. Listen to the sounds of the mechanisms in the door operating as the door knob turns and you are allowed entry. Slowly open the door.

As you enter through the doorway you find yourself in a large garden. It is filled with beautiful, lush and colorful plant life. Amidst this garden are people. But these people have a different glow to them than the people you would normally encounter. They appear to be bright and almost translucent. They look at you and smile, but no one approaches you as you walk into the garden. You notice that you are feeling quite safe and protected amongst these people. You seem to be existing as they exist. Every fiber of your being is relaxed and calm as you pass along the pathways of the garden and enjoy the scenery in the company of your translucent companions.

Suddenly, you come upon a translucent woman who was unaware of your presence and she jumps in a startled fashion. You reach out to her to calm her and assure her that you mean no harm. You smile as she regains her composure, smiles back at you and continues on with what she was doing. This experiences brings a new light to your situation. You are left with the distinct impression that these translucent people can be just as started by your presence as you could be by theirs.

You suddenly feel very compassionate for these translucent people. You recognize that they are people who have left their dense bodies behind, but have retained their other faculties. You are very similar. You notice that you have no fear while walking amongst them and you wonder why you ever had fear in the past. You realize that you have been co-existing with them right along and that there is no need to be fearful from them. You also realize that they have retained their personalities and therefore, should you encounter one in the future you would deal with him or her and address him or her in the same manner as you would a human being who you might encounter on the street. There is no difference. Just as humans have personalities, you recognize that these ghosts have personalities as well. Because of this, you understand that they will vary in their response to meeting you just as a human being would vary in his response to meeting you. All fear leaves you with this new awareness. This new awakening and discovery. You are excited at the concept of co-existing. You are comforted with the concept of live and let live.

You are now going to leave the garden through the gilded doorway. You can take one last look at your new friends and say good-bye if you wish. Now, close the door slowly and walk back down the corridor to the bottom of the stairway. I'm going to count from one to twenty. As I count from one to twenty you will begin to climb back up the stairway. As I count from one to twenty and you climb back up the stairway you will feel more and more alert and more and more refreshed. When I count the number twenty you will open your eyes, feeling wide awake...very alert and ready to continue with your day.

Meeting Your Spirit Guide

Relax your body, relax your mind... relax... relax.. as you listen to my voice and only to my voice...relax your body and relax your mind... relax... relax... as you listen to my voice and only to my voice. Breathe in slowly... as you exhale... all pain and darkness is released with the stale old air. Breathe in to the count of eight and out to the count of ten.

Now that you are feeling relaxed and calm, visualize a stairwell ... a very well lit stairwell. Now, see yourself walking down the stairwell. You may not see me near you, but know that I am with you while you walk down the stair well. Watch your feet as you walk down the stairwell. There is a railing that you can hang onto if you choose to do so. And as you walk down the stairwell I am going to count from twenty to one. With every number that I count, you will walk now one more tread. When I reach number one, you will be at the bottom of the stairwell. Let's begin... 20...19..18.. (etc.)

Now that you are at the bottom of the stairwell, you see before you a long corridor. Walk to the end of the corridor. When you reach the end of the corridor, you will see a beautiful gilded doorway with a beautiful golden door knob. Place your hand on the golden door knob and turn it slowly. Listen to the sounds of the mechanisms in the door operating as the door knob turns and you are allowed entry. Slowly open the door.

Walk through the doorway. As you walk through the doorway you will find yourself in your favorite place. This is a place that you and only you are aware of. This is a place where you feel safe and secure. This is a place where nothing can harm you.

In your favorite place you have a favorite spot where you like to sit. Go there and sit. Feel your body relax and release all tension as you are filled with trust and love in your favorite, safe and protective place.

As you breath in a deep and relaxed manner, you see someone approaching you. The image is vague at first, but slowly comes into clarity. This image is your spirit guide. You sense and feel the love coming toward you from this guide and you know instinctively that your guide is there in love only.

A sense of comradeship overtakes you as your guide approaches. You recognize that you are a team. You recognize that your guide is just that, a guide. Someone to assist you through

The preceding inductions are just a few of the many hundreds of inductions that can be performed to assist you or your clients on a journey toward a more complete and balanced lifestyle. Please use these inductions as a foundation to give you ideas on adapting them to other unique situations (or common) that you may find yourself facing.

About the Author

Born in upstate New York, Rev. Lena Sheehan began her studies of holistic care of body, mind and spirit in 1983. She now holds a diploma in Naturopathy, is a member of the American Association of Professional Hypnotherapists, a Nutrition Specialist and Emotional Release Therapy (ERT). She is a (fifth generation from Mrs. Takata) Reiki Mater Teacher, a Karuna Ki Master Teacher and a Master Teacher of Haymanootha Healing.

On the spiritual side of things, Rev. Lena Sheehan is an ordained minister and a director of ministries for the Universal Brotherhood Movement and was also ordained by Dr. Willard Fuller into the evangelistic ministry of the Lively Stones Fellowship. She is a medical intuitive as well as a spiritist, spiritual consultant, spiritual life and business coach and an animal communicator.

Rev. Sheehan shares her knowledge and talents, not only with private clients for personal, business and medical matters, but in occasional radio appearances, lectures and workshops with groups such as Hospice and adult education classes at the local college. She has created several distance courses as well.

Another Great Self-Help Book
by Rev. Lena Sheehan!

Natural Solutions for Stress of Body, Mind & Spirit
ISBN: 978-0-9820562-2-6

Read more about it at:
www.raularpublishing.com

Printed in the United Kingdom by
Lightning Source UK Ltd., Milton Keynes
139822UK00001B/77/P